T0184149

Communications
in Computer and Information Science   1636

More information about this series at https://link.springer.com/bookseries/7899

Byeong-Yun Chang · Changbeom Choi (Eds.)

Methods and Applications for Modeling and Simulation of Complex Systems

20th Asian Simulation Conference, AsiaSim 2021
Virtual Event, November 17–20, 2021
Proceedings

Springer

Editors
Byeong-Yun Chang
Ajou University
Suwon, Korea (Republic of)

Changbeom Choi ⓘ
Hanbat National University
Daejeon, Korea (Republic of)

ISSN 1865-0929 ISSN 1865-0937 (electronic)
Communications in Computer and Information Science
ISBN 978-981-19-6856-3 ISBN 978-981-19-6857-0 (eBook)
https://doi.org/10.1007/978-981-19-6857-0

This Springer imprint is published by the registered company Springer Nature Singapore Pte Ltd.
The registered company address is: 152 Beach Road, #21-01/04 Gateway East, Singapore 189721, Singapore

Preface

The Asian Simulation Conference (AsiaSim) started in 2001 and has been organized by KSS (Korea Society for Simulation), SSAGsg (Society of Simulation and Gaming of Singapore), JSST (Japan Society for Simulation Technology), CSF (China Simulation Federation), and MSS (Malaysian Simulation Society) as an academic event representing Asia. AsiaSim is an event where experts in modeling and simulation from various fields in Asia gather to share research results and broaden relationships.

AsiaSim is an annual academic event, but unfortunately, the conference could not be held in 2020 due to the COVID-19 pandemic. However, in 2021, AsiaSim was held in the metaverse, where modeling and simulation technology is the basis of the service. In the metaverse, every participant experienced convergence between the real world and the virtual world.

Research results on various topics, from modeling and simulation theory to manufacturing, defense, transportation, and general engineering fields that combine simulation with computer graphics simulations, were shared at the AsiaSim 2021 academic event venue built in the metaverse. Three reviewers evaluated each contribution. A total of 19 papers were presented in the oral session, and four were presented in the poster session. Among them, only nine papers were finally accepted for this CCIS volume.

We thank the keynote speakers, David Goldsman, Byunghee Kim, Lin Zhang, and Satoshi Tanaka, for giving great insights to the attendees. Furthermore, we wish to thank the external reviewers for their time, effort, and timely response. Also, we thank the Program Committee and Organizing Committee members who made the conference successful. Finally, we thank the participants who participated remotely despite the difficult circumstances.

July 2022

Byeong-Yun Chang
Changbeom Choi

Organization

Honorary Chairs

Sung Jo Hong	Dongguk University, South Korea
Yun Bae Kim	Sungkyunkwan University, South Korea
Axel Lehmann	Universität de Bundeswehr München, Germany

General Chair

Byeong-Yun Chang	Ajou University, South Korea

General Co-chairs

Bo Hu Li (President of CSF)	Beihang University, China
Kazuo Furuta (President of JSST)	University of Tokyo, Japan
Yahaya Md Sam (President of MSS)	Universiti Teknologi Malaysia, Malaysia
Gary Tan (President of AsiaSim and President of SSAGSG)	National University of Singapore, Singapore

Program Chair

Changbeom Choi	Hanbat National University, South Korea

Organizing Committee

Jinsoo Park	Yong In University, South Korea
Heesuk Seo	Korea University of Technology Education, South Korea
Se Won Lee	Pukyong National University, South Korea

Publication Committee

Jonghun Lee	Daegu Gyeongbuk Institute of Science and Technology, South Korea
Jung Wook Baek	Chosun University, South Korea
Hae Young Lee	Cheongju University, South Korea
Yongwhan Park	Yeungnam University, South Korea
Sang Ahn Kim	Siena College, South Korea

Jong-ho Shin	Chosun University, South Korea
Jin Myoung Kim	Ministry of National Defense, South Korea
Su Man Nam	DuDuIT, South Korea
Gyu M. Lee	Pusan National University, South Korea

Industrial Committee

Jonghun Lee	Daegu Gyeongbuk Institute of Science and Technology, South Korea
Sang Dong Kim	Daegu Gyeongbuk Institute of Science and Technology, South Korea
Jeong Tak Ryu	Daegu University, South Korea
Young Suk Park	Atworth Co., Ltd., South Korea
Ku-kil Chang	Dassault Systemes Korea, South Korea
Young Gyo Chung	SimTech Systems, Inc., South Korea
Seong-Hoon Choi	Sangmyung University, South Korea

Award Committee

Dong-Won Seo	Kyung Hee University, South Korea
Hyung Jong Kim	Seoul Women's University, South Korea
Byungjoo Park	Hannam University, South Korea
Sungsu Kim	Kyungpook National University, South Korea
Seung Hyun Yoon	Electronics and Telecommunications Research Institute, South Korea
Jiyeon Kim	Seoul Women's University, South Korea
Jin Hyung Kim	Korea Internet & Security Agency, South Korea
Eun Young Jang	LG Uplus Corp., South Korea

International Program Committee

Changbeom Choi	Hanbat National University, South Korea
Sooyoung Jang	Electronics and Telecommunications Research Institute, South Korea
Kyung-Min Seo	Korea University of Technology Education, South Korea
Jangwon Bae	Korea University of Technology Education, South Korea
Kyoungchan Won	Center for Army Analysis & Simulation, South Korea
Gyu M. Lee	Pusan National University, South Korea
Bohu Li	Beijing University of Aeronautics and Astronautics, China

Liang Li	Ritsumeikan University, Japan
Satoshi Tanaka	Ritsumeikan University, Japan
Lin Zhang	Beihang University, China
Terence Hung	Rolls Royce, Singapore
Dong Jin	Illinois Institute of Technology, USA
Farzad Kamrani	KTH Royal Institute of Technology, Sweden
Helen Karatza	Aristotle University of Thessaloniki, Greece
Sye Loong Keoh	University of Glasgow, Singapore, Singapore
Yun Bae Kim	Sungkyunkwan University, South Korea
Ge Li	National University of Defence Technology, China
Zengxiang Li	Institute of High Performance Computing, A*STAR, Singapore
Malcolm Low	Singapore Institute of Technology, Singapore
Linbo Luo	Xidian University, China
Imran Mahmood	National University of Sciences & Technology, Pakistan
Yahaya Md Sam	Universiti Teknologi Malaysia, Malaysia
Zaharuddin Mohamed	Universiti Teknologi Malaysia, Malaysia
Navonil Mustafee	University of Exeter, UK
Bhakti Stephan Onggo	University of Southampton, UK
Ravi Seshadri	Singapore-MIT Alliance for Research and Technology, Singapore
Xiao Song	Beihang University, China
Yuen Jien Soo	National University of Singapore, Singapore
Claudia Szabo	University of Adelaide, Australia
Sun Teck Tan	National University of Singapore, Singapore
Wenjie Tang	National University of Defense Technology, China
Yifa Tang	Chinese Academy of Sciences, China
Simon Taylor	Brunel University, UK
Yong Meng Teo	National University of Singapore, Singapore
Georgios Theodoropoulos	Southern University of Science and Technology, China
Stephen John Turner	Vidyasirimedhi Institute of Science and Technology, Thailand
Bimlesh Wadhwa	National University of Singapore, Singapore
Yiping Yao	National University of Defense Technology, China
Allan N. Zhang	Singapore Institute of Manufacturing Technology, Singapore
Jinghui Zhong	South China University of Technology, China

Additional Reviewers

Kangsun Lee
Jun-Gyu Kang
Seon Han Choi
Sang-Hwan Kim
Nam-Su Ahn
Jinho Lee
Heungseob Kim

Dohyung Kim
Sangjin Lee
Junghoon Kim
Kyungtae Lim
Taehoon Kim
Haneol Jang

Contents

Simulation and Visualization

Toward Agent-Based In Situ Visualization

Yan Wang[1]([⊠])[ID], Ren Sakai[2][ID], and Akira Kageyama[3][ID]

[1] Graduate School of System Informatics, Kobe University, Kobe 657-8501, Japan
190x701x@stu.kobe-u.ac.jp
[2] Faculty of Engineering, Kobe University, Kobe 657-8501, Japan
[3] Graduate School of System Informatics, Kobe University, Kobe 657-8501, Japan

Abstract. In situ visualization is becoming an essential method used for high-performance computing. For effective in situ visualization, a viewpoint should be placed close to a key spot or volume-of-interest (VOI). In order to track unpredictable motions of VOI in simulations, we propose to introduce agent-based modeling to the in-situ visualization, in which agents are autonomous cameras, and their environment is the simulation. As a demonstration experiment of the agent-based in situ visualization, we put a camera agent to 3D cellular automata. The camera agent successfully tracks a VOI of cells in highly complex time development.

Keywords: HPC · In situ visualization · Agent-based model · Agent-based visualization · Cellular automata

1 Introduction

In situ visualization is becoming an important research topic in high-performance computing (HPC), because it enables the analysis of simulation data without reducing the spatiotemporal resolution [7]. One challenge with in situ visualization is the method used to identify a local critical region in the whole simulation space, or volume of interest (VOI), where intensive visualizations are to be applied. In large-scale computer simulations of complex phenomena, however, it is almost impossible to know in advance when and where essential phenomena will occur.

In 2014, we proposed an in situ visualization approach that enables interactive analysis of VOI after simulation [14]. The key idea is to apply multiple in situ visualizations from fixed viewpoints at once before applying the interactive exploration of video dataset on PCs. (We focus on 3D simulations with time development.) The visualization cameras for recording of the video dataset were assumed to be primarily placed on 2D surfaces such as a sphere. Similar approach based on images to in situ visualization is Cinema [1,20].

By generalizing our video-based method, we proposed "4D Street View" [12, 13], where we placed omnidirectional cameras using a full ($=4\pi$ steradians) field of view. The omnidirectional cameras are placed in various forms in the simulation region such as on curves (1D), on surfaces (2D), or in the whole simulation region (3D). The viewpoint and viewing direction can be interactively changed

B.-Y. Chang and C. Choi (Eds.): AsiaSim 2021, CCIS 1636, pp. 3–10, 2022.
https://doi.org/10.1007/978-981-19-6857-0_1

afterward as in the Google street view [2] using an application program for PC, called 4D street viewer.

This study proposes another complementary approach to in situ visualizations to focus on VOI. It enables automatic tracking of the unpredictable behavior of VOI, such as sudden emergence/disappearance and random motion. This is achieved by integrating the agent-based model (ABM) into in situ visualizations. In this agent-based in situ visualization, agents are visualization cameras, and they autonomously identify and track VOI by following prescribed rules and applying in situ visualizations.

Our long-term goal is to implement the agent-based in situ visualization as a set of visualization cameras or "camera swarm". Toward the goal, this study presents a single camera as an element of the autonomous camera agent.

2   Related Work

Multiple in situ visualization approaches for HPC have been proposed. Temporal caching [9] is to temporarily store simulation outputs in a fast storage system for later events triggered based on the stored data. The particle data approach [15] saves view-independent particle data for the later application of particle-based rendering [21]. Proxy image [26,27,32] is a method that uses the intermediate representation of data.

Several libraries and frameworks for in situ HPC visualization have been developed, including ParaView Catalyst [3], VisIt libsim [30], ISAAC [17], Embree [29], OSPray [28], and VISMO [18,19]. ADIOS [16] is an adaptable data I/O framework, enabling asynchronous communication between simulation and visualization. SENSEI [4] is a generic in situ interface, providing a portable interface for other in situ infrastructures such as Catalyst, libsim, and OSPray.

The application of ABM to information visualization in general was proposed by [11]. They coined the term agent-based visualization (ABV). The agent-based in situ visualization proposed in this study is an application of ABV to in situ visualization for HPC.

In computer graphics, the automatic setting of camera path is an important topic having a long history [8,10,25]. Here, a relatively simple algorithm for the camera agent motion is used because the camera agent is required to autonomously respond to ever-changing simulation data.

3   Camera Agent

In general, an ABM consists of two components; environment and autonomous entities called agents [31]. Each agent interacts with the environment and other agents, following simple rules. For our proposed agent-based visualization, an agent is a visualization camera that autonomously changes its position and viewing direction. Unlike the omnidirectional cameras scattered in the 4D street view, the agent camera is directional one with a smaller field-of-view than 4π steradians. The environment is the simulation space and the physical variables

distributed there. The camera is designed to track VOI and visualize the phenomena therein. Here we focus on the behavior of a single agent.

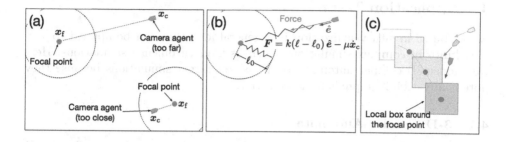

Fig. 1. (a) The agent is pulled or pushed as per the distance to its (fixed) focal point.
(b) The agent moves following the mass-spring-damper model. (c) The focal point in
the next time step is re-calculated from local environment around it (local box).

Figure 1 shows the rules for camera-agent motion: (i) First, the agent calculates the center of VOI called focal point from the environment [the red points
in (a)]; (ii) If the distance to the focal point is larger than a reference length ℓ_0,
the camera agent is then pulled to the focal point; (iii) Otherwise, the agent is
pushed away from the focal point.

To implement rules (ii) and (iii), we adopt a simple mass-spring-damper
model with dual time stepping. The camera agent follows an equation of motion
with its intrinsic time τ, which is independent from simulation's time t. Assuming
that the mass of the agent $m = 1$, we adopt the equation of motion for the
position vector of the camera agent $\boldsymbol{x}_c$ as follows [Fig. 1(b)]:

$$\frac{d^2 \boldsymbol{x}_c}{d\tau^2} = k(\ell - \ell_0)\,\hat{e} - \mu \frac{d\boldsymbol{x}_c}{d\tau}, \tag{1}$$

where k and μ are spring constant and friction coefficient; ℓ is the distance
between the focal point $\boldsymbol{x}_f$ and the camera agent, or $\ell = |\boldsymbol{x}_f - \boldsymbol{x}_c|$; and $\hat{e}$ is unit
vector $\hat{e} = (\boldsymbol{x}_f - \boldsymbol{x}_c)/\ell$. We numerically integrate Eq. (1) for τ, assuming that
the focal point $\boldsymbol{x}_f$ is fixed during the integration. In other words, time t stops
during the τ's integration. On the other hand, the focal point moves according
to the environmental change, or the development of the simulation in t, while
the motion of the agent by Eq. (1) is suspended. We alternately apply the dual
time integrations. We set ℓ_0, a free parameter in this method, as $\ell_0 = 30$, with
the unit length being the cell size.

The camera agent assumes a part (or sometimes all) of the simulation region
called local box, which is defined around the focal point [Fig. 1(c)]. As the environment changes (or as the simulation progresses in time t), the local box range,
and accordingly its central focal point, moves. According to the above procedure,
the camera agent smoothly tracks the motion of VOI, almost always keeping the
appropriate distance ℓ_0 [Fig. 1(c)]. The VOI tracked by the camera agent depends

on the initial position of the agent. This uncertainty of VOI will be resolved if we introduce multiple agents in future.

4   Application Tests

Agent-based in situ visualization is a general idea that can be applied to various kinds of complex simulations, such as fluid turbulence simulations. Here we choose 3D cellular automata (CA) as test target simulations because they potentially exhibit unpredictable behavior.

4.1   3-D Cellular Automata

We consider 3D cartesian lattice cells with discrete (integer) states and a simple ruleset to change the states in the next time step. The rules are local, i.e., the next state of a cell is determined by its state and that of its neighbors. CA is known to mimic complex phenomena observed in nature [24]. The complex time evolution of 3D CA described below makes them suitable applications of the proposed agent-based in situ visualization method.

In the following, we call a cell empty, when its state $= 0$, and alive when its state $= 1$. The total number of possible states is n: The state of a cell is one of $\{0, 1, 2, \ldots, n - 1\}$. The total number of alive cells in neighbors is m.

We adopt the $Rule\,[\alpha/\beta/n/\gamma]$ notation to specify a CA rule set, where α is an integer or a set of integers for m to make an empty cell alive (born); β is an integer or a set of integers for m to keep an alive cell being alive; and γ is either N (Neumann neighbor) or M (Moore neighbor). When m does not match α (when the cell is empty) or β (when the cell is alive), or the cell is neither alive nor empty (state > 1), 1 is added to the state integer modulo n. We will present the situ visualizations of $Rule\,[4/4/5/M]$ and $Rule\,[5/4, 5/2/M]$ below.

We developed a 3D CA code in C++ and incorporated the in situ visualization function using a single camera agent in the code. Our simulation code executes any CA model described by the $Rule[\alpha/\beta/n/\gamma]$ with periodic boundary conditions in all three (x, y, and z) directions. The program is assumed to be executed on a supercomputer system as a batch job. Although the code is not parallelized, it will be done soon.

We place spheres at non-empty cells and the sphere color depends on the state integer of the cell. Kyoto Visualization System (KVS) [22], which is a visualization development framework for C++, was employed for the in-situ rendering of the spheres on π-computer system of Kobe University, comprising 16 nodes of AMD APYC CPU (512 cores in total). Results of the in situ visualization or the output of KVS are stored as a sequence of image files on the hard disk drive system. These images are then combined into a video file playable on PCs.

4.2   CA of $Rule\,[4/4/5/M]$

First, we demonstrate the results of in situ visualization of CA with $Rule[4/4/5/M]$, which leads to highly complicated dynamics of cells. We could not find literatures describing this CA. We recommend a YouTube video [23] to comprehend the brilliant and impressive developments of cells. The *Rule* [4/4/5/M] appears at the beginning of the video.

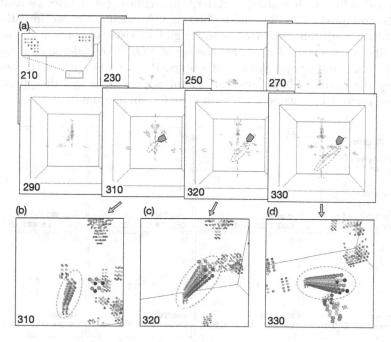

Fig. 2. (a) Snapshots of a 3-D CA. Two clusters collide after 210 time steps and highly complicated structures are then observed. Observe that a camera agent (schematically shown by the blue glyph) tracks a bar-like object (enclosed by a magenta curve). (b), (c), and (d) are images of in the situ visualization by the camera agent. (Color figure online)

Figure 2(a) shows a sequence of snapshots of the CA from 210–330 steps. The cell lattice size is $100 \times 100 \times 100$. At 210 steps, two clusters of non-empty cells are observed (magnified view in the blue box). They collide later and break in multiple fragments at 230 steps. Then, the scattered fragments undergo additional mutual collisions from 250 steps and above. At the 310th step, we observe an emergence of rod-like structures (enclosed by the magenta-dashed line).

Here we define VOI as the center of gravity of alive cells in the local box. When there is no alive cell in the local box, the camera agent does not move, waiting for a change. When a cluster of cells goes into the local box, the camera agent notices its entrance and starts tracking (green glyph in Fig. 2(a)). The viewing direction is toward the center of gravity. In spite of its simplicity, the rule enables the camera agent to follow a bar-like object, as shown in Figs. 2(b), (c), and (d).

4.3 CA of *Rule* [5/4, 5/2/M]

The second example of CA to which the agent-based in situ visualization is applied is *Rule* [5/4, 5/2/M]. This CA is one of the extensions of Conway's game of life in 3-D [5, 6], which enables a "glider," an oscillating structure of a relatively few cells, to translate in the space. In this CA calculation, we intentionally set an initial condition, such that a single glider exists, to confirm the agent's trackability in the event of a sudden change of VOI. The glider goes through a boundary plane and re-appears from the opposite plane because of the periodic boundary conditions. These kinds of abrupt appearances and disappearances should be tracked by a camera agent in complex simulations.

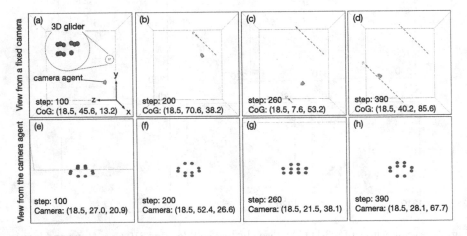

Fig. 3. Agent-based in situ visualization of 3D game of life. (a)–(d): A glider moves in the simulation region under the periodic boundary condition and a camera agent (green glyph) tracks the glider. (e)–(h): Images taken by the camera agent. The cell size is 70 × 80 × 90. (Color figure online)

Figures 3(a)–(d) show the glider's translation (a group of purple cells). The blue arrow denotes the glider trajectory. The green glyph shows the position of the camera agent. (The blue arrow and green glyph are shown for the explanation, they do not appear in the CA computation.) The agent notices the disappearance and appearance of the glider after (b) and before (c), respectively. The successful tracking of the glider's "teleportations" subsequently continues after (d).

Figures 3(e)–(h) show images obtained by the camera agent's in situ visualization at designated time steps corresponding (a)–(d). The glider is recorded at the center of the images, as shown in these figures.

5 Summary

We propose agent-based in situ visualization for effective in situ visualization of HPC. Toward the full capacity of agent-based modeling of visualization cameras, we developed a single camera agent in this paper. We have shown that the camera agent autonomously tracks VOI in 3D CA, applying in situ visualizations of the VOI during a batch job simulation on an HPC system. Based on the single agent proposed in this paper, we will study multiple agents in the future, expecting the emergence of collective order as observed in general ABMs.

The agent-based in situ visualization is complementary to the omnidirectional stationary cameras in the 4D street view. For the effective analysis of HPC data, we will combine autonomous camera agents and omnidirectional stationary cameras in the future studies.

Acknowledgments. This work was supported by Grant-in-Aid for Scientific Research (KAKENHI) 17H02998. We thank Dr. Naohisa Sakamoto for valuable technical advice and for fruitful discussions.

References

1. Ahrens, J., et al.: In Situ MPAS-ocean image-based visualization. In: SC14 International Conference for High Performance Computing, Networking, Storage and Analysis, pp. 3–6 (2014)
2. Anguelov, D., et al.: Google street view: capturing the world at street level. Comput. (Long. Beach. Calif). **43**(6), 32–38 (2010)
3. Ayachit, U., et al.: ParaView catalyst. In: Proceedings of First Work. Situ Infrastructures Enabling Extreme-Scale Analysis and Visualization - ISAV2015, pp. 25–29. ACM Press (2015)
4. Ayachit, U., et al.: The SENSEI generic in situ interface. In: Proceedings of ISAV 2016 2nd Working Situ Infrastructures Enabling Extreme - Held Conjunction with SC 2016 International Conference High Performance Computing Networking, Storage Analysis, pp. 40–44 (2017)
5. Bays, C.: Candidates for the game of life in three dimensions. Complex Syst. **1**, 373–400 (1987)
6. Bays, C.: A note about the discovery of many new rules for the game of three-dimensional life. Complex Syst. **16**, 381–386 (2006). http://www.cse.sc.edu/bays/CAhomePage
7. Bennett, J.C., Childs, H., Garth, C., Hentschel, B.: In Situ Visualization for Computational Science. vol. 18271, pp. 1–43. Springer, Cham (2018). https://doi.org/10.1007/978-3-030-81627-8
8. Chen, Z., Zhou, J., Sun, R., Kang, L.: A new evolving mechanism of genetic algorithm for multi-constraint intelligent camera path planning. Soft Comput. **25**(7), 5073–5092 (2021). https://doi.org/10.1007/s00500-020-05510-6
9. Demarle, D.E., Bauer, A.: In situ visualization with temporal caching. Comput. Sci. Eng. **23**, 25–33 (2021)
10. Drucker, S.M., Zeltzer, D.: Intelligent camera control in a virtual environment. In: Graph. Interface 1994, pp. 190–199. Banff, Canada (1994)
11. Grignard, A., Drogoul, A.: Agent-based visualization: a real-time visualization tool applied both to data and simulation outputs. In: AAAI-17 Workshops Human-Machine Collaborative Learning, pp. 670–675 (2017)
12. Kageyama, A., Sakamoto, N.: 4D street view: a video-based visualization method. Peer J. Comput. Sci. **6**, e305 (2020)
13. Kageyama, A., Sakamoto, N., Miura, H., Ohno, N.: Interactive exploration of the in-situ visualization of a magnetohydrodynamic simulation. Plasma Fusion Res. **15**, 1401065 (2020)

14. Kageyama, A., Yamada, T.: An approach to exascale visualization: interactive viewing of in-situ visualization. Comput. Phys. Commun. **185**, 79–85 (2014)
15. Kawamura, T., Noda, T., Idomura, Y.: In-situ visual exploration of multivariate volume data based on particle based volume rendering. In: 2nd Workshops of Situ Infrastructures Enabling Extreming Analysis and Visualization, pp. 18–22 (2016)
16. Lofstead, J., Klasky, S., Schwan, K., Podhorszki, N., Jin, C.: Flexible IO and integration for scientific codes through the adaptable IO system (ADIOS). In: Proceedings of 6th International Workshops on Challenges Large Applications Distribution Environments, pp. 15–24 (2008)
17. Matthes, A., Huebl, A., Widera, R., Grottel, S., Gumhold, S., Bussmann, M.: In situ, steerable, hardware-independent and data-structure agnostic visualization with ISAAC. Supercomput. Front. Innov. **3**(4), 30–48 (2016)
18. Ohno, N., Kageyama, A.: In-situ visualization library for Yin-Yang grid simulations. Earth, Planet Space. **73**, 158 (2021)
19. Ohno, N., Ohtani, H.: Development of in-situ visualization tool for PIC simulation. Plasma Fusion Res. **9**, 341071 (2014)
20. O'Leary, P., Ahrens, J., Jourdain, S., Wittenburg, S., Rogers, D.H., Petersen, M.: Cinema image-based in situ analysis and visualization of MPAS-ocean simulations. Parallel Comput. **55**, 43–48 (2016)
21. Sakamoto, N., Nonaka, J., Koyamada, K., Tanaka, S.: Particle-based volume rendering. In: 6th International Asia-Pacific Symposium and Visualization, pp. 129–132. IEEE, February 2007
22. Sakamoto, N., Koyamada, K.: KVS: a simple and effective framework for scientific visualization. J. Adv. Simul. Sci. Eng. **2**, 76–95 (2015)
23. Softology: 3D Cellular Automata. http://www.youtube.com/watch?v=dQJ5aEs P6Fs
24. Wolfram, S.: A New Kind of Science. Wolfram Media, Champaign (2002)
25. Tharwat, A., Elhoseny, M., Hassanien, A.E., Gabel, T., Kumar, A.: Intelligent Bézier curve-based path planning model using chaotic particle swarm optimization algorithm. Cluster Comput. **22**(2), 4745–4766 (2018). https://doi.org/10.1007/s10586-018-2360-3
26. Tikhonova, A., Correa, C.D., Kwan-Liu, M.: Explorable images for visualizing volume data. In: Proceedings of IEEE Pacific Visualization Symposium 2010, PacificVis 2010, pp. 177–184 (2010)
27. Tikhonova, A., Correa, C.D., Ma, K.L.: Visualization by proxy: a novel framework for deferred interaction with volume data. IEEE Trans. Vis. Comput. Graph. **16**(6), 1551–1559 (2010)
28. Wald, I., et al.: OSPRay - a CPU ray tracing framework for scientific visualization. IEEE Trans. Vis. Comput. Graph. **23**(1), 931–940 (2017)
29. Wald, I., Woop, S., Benthin, C., Johnson, G.S., Ernst, M.: Embree: a kernel framework for efficient CPU ray tracing. ACM Trans. Graph. **33**(4), 8 (2014)
30. Whitlock, B., Favre, M.J., Meredith, S.J.: Parallel in situ coupling of simulation with a fully featured visualization system. In: Eurographics Symposium on Parallel Graphics and Visualization, pp. 101–109 (2011)
31. Wilensky, U., Rand, W.: An Introduction to Agent-based Modeling : Modeling Natural, Social, and Engineered Complex Systems with NetLogo. MIT Press, Cambridge (2015)
32. Ye, Y., Miller, R., Ma, K.L.: In situ pathtube visualization with explorable images. In: 13th Eurographics Symposium on Parallel Graphics and Visualization, pp. 9–16. Eurographics Association (2013)

Application of the Edge Upsampling Network to Soft-Edge Regions in a 3D-Scanned Point Cloud

Weite Li[1]([✉]), Kyoko Hasegawa[2], Liang Li[2], Akihiro Tsukamoto[3],
Yamaguchi Hiroshi[4], Fadjar I. Thufail[5], Brahmantara[6], and Satoshi Tanaka[2]

[1] Graduate School of Information Science and Engineering, Ritsumeikan University,
Shiga, Japan
wtli@ctbu.edu.cn
[2] College of Information Science and Engineering, Ritsumeikan University, Shiga, Japan
[3] Graduate School of Integrated Arts and Sciences, Tokushima University, Tokushima, Japan
[4] Nara National Research Institute for Cultural Properties, Nara, Japan
[5] Research Center for Area Studies (P2W), Indonesian Institute of Sciences (LIPI),
Jakarta, Indonesia
[6] Borobudur Conservation Office, Magelang, Indonesia

Abstract. Large-scale 3D scanning data based on point clouds enable accurate
and fast recording of complex objects in the real world. The edges in a scanned
point cloud usually describe the complex 3D structure of the target object and the
surrounding scene. The recently proposed deep learning-based edge upsampling
network can generate new points in the edge regions. When combined with the
edge-highlighted transparent visualization method, this network can effectively
improve the visibility of the edge regions in 3D-scanned point clouds. However,
most previous upsampling experiments were performed on the sharp-edge regions
despite that 3D-scanned objects usually contain both sharp and soft edge regions.
In this paper, to demonstrate the performance of the upsampling network on soft-
edge regions, we add more polygon models that contain soft edges by adjusting the
models in the training set so that the network can learn more features of soft-edge
regions. Additionally, we apply the upsampling network to real 3D-scanned point
cloud data that contain numerous soft edges to verify that the edge upsampling
network is equally effective at the upsampling task on soft-edge regions. The
experimental results show that the visibility of the complex 3D-scanned objects
can be effectively improved by increasing the point density in the soft-edge regions.

Keywords: Point upsampling · 3D-scanned point cloud · Transparent
visualization

1 Introduction

The development of 3D scanning technology in recent years has made it possible to
precisely record complex objects in the real world. To observe the internal structure
and external contours of complex objects more intuitively, we proposed opacity-based

B.-Y. Chang and C. Choi (Eds.): AsiaSim 2021, CCIS 1636, pp. 11–18, 2022.
https://doi.org/10.1007/978-981-19-6857-0_2

edge highlighting [1], which combines the edge-highlighting technique with transparent visualization based on stochastic point-based rendering (SPBR) [2, 3] to highlight 3D edges, which substantially improves the transparent visibility of complex objects. However, the points in the 3D-scanned point cloud data are not always dense and uniform along the edges, and the point density in the edge regions tends to be low due to errors in the measurement and edge extraction process. Yu et al. [4] proposed a deep learning-based upsampling network for sparse point cloud data. However, this approach is usually applied to the upsampling task of overall point clouds. Therefore, to improve the visibility of edge regions, we proposed a deep learning-based network [5] for upsampling edge points. This network can improve the transparent visualization visibility of edge regions in complex 3D-scanned objects. In fact, in real 3D-scanned objects, the edges are usually divided into sharp edge and soft-edge regions. In our previous work [5], we applied the proposed network mainly to sharp edges and obtained excellent results. In addition, we also made a preliminary discussion on the possibility of applying the proposed network to soft edges. This paper is a further development of our previous work. We focus on applying the proposed network to 3D-scanned point cloud data that contain numerous soft-edge regions and demonstrate the applicability to soft edges. By adjusting the models in the training set, the network can learn more features of the soft-edge regions to generate more understandable soft edges and improve the visibility.

2 Methods

2.1 Opacity-Based Edge Highlighting of Soft Edges

To extract 3D edges, i.e., high-curvature areas, of the target point cloud, we adopt the statistical method [6–8], which uses an appropriate eigenvalue-based 3D feature value. For a local spherical region centered at each point, the variances and covariances of point distributions are numerically calculated, and the local 3D structure tensor [9] is defined. Then, the 3D feature value is calculated using the tensor's three eigenvalues, and the value is assigned to the centered point. The 3D edges are extracted by collecting points with large feature values. In our work, we adopt change-of-curvature as the feature value $f : f = \lambda_3/(\lambda_1 + \lambda_2 + \lambda_3)$ with $\lambda_i (i = 1, 2, 3, \lambda_1 \geq \lambda_2 \geq \lambda_3 \geq 0)$, the three eigenvalues of the 3D structure tensor.

Recently, we proposed opacity-based edge highlighting applicable to 3D scanned point clouds [1]. The idea is to execute transparent visualization of the target point cloud and assign larger opacity to the extracted 3D edges regions. We can increase the edge opacity by locally increasing the point density using upsampling and applying stochastic point-based rendering (SPBR) [2, 3], in which regions with higher point density are visualized with larger opacity.

The difficulty in highlighting the soft edges is that there are no sharp peak regions of the feature value f. The value of f gradually increases around the soft edges, and a "feature-value gradation" appears. In such soft-edge regions, introducing a definite feature-value threshold is not easy, aiming at distinguishing the edge regions from the remaining non-edge regions. Therefore, we rather consider an intermediate area where the feature-value gradation occurs. Then, we make the feature-value gradation correspond to the "opacity gradation" based on the opacity formula of SPBR [1]. In the created image, the opacity gradation appears as a "brightness gradation" that shows the existence of the soft edges.

The contribution of the current paper is proposing a deep learning-based high-quality upsampling of the soft-edge regions. For sharp edges, upsampling by simple copying the original points works well [1]. However, for soft edges, we need more careful upsampling so that the delicate opacity gradation can be correctly reflected in the edge-highlighting visualization.

2.2 Proposed Upsampling Network

In our work, we aim to upsample the edge regions in 3D scanned point clouds. In our training phase, we adopt training strategies similar to [4], which use polygon data to generate high-precision point cloud data for training. However, in contrast to our previous work [5], we add 10 polygon mesh models containing numerous soft edges to the training set and remove 10 models that only contain sharp edges to achieve better upsampling performance in the soft-edge regions. Specifically, we cut each polygon mesh data used for training to generate numerous local patches. To generate training point cloud data with a uniform point distribution and fine detail retention, Poisson disk sampling (PDS) [10] is used to generate points on these patches as ground truth $\mathcal{T}$. Then, the ground truth data are downsampled to generate sparse input point cloud data $\mathcal{P} = \{p_i \in \mathbb{R}^{3\times1}\}_{i=1}^{N}$ with N points. As illustrated in Fig. 1, the network consists of a generator and a discriminator, and the discriminator guides the generator training. Continuous adversarial training alternating between the two models eventually makes

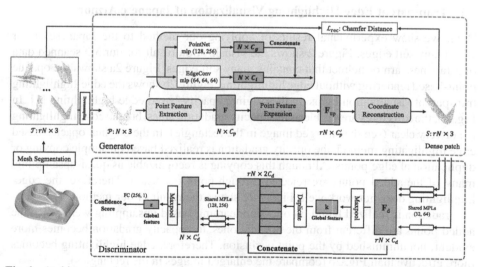

Fig. 1. Architecture of the proposed upsampling network. Note that N is the number of points in input patch $\mathcal{P}$, and r is the upsampling rate. Given a sparse input patch $\mathcal{P}$ with N points, we generate a dense patch S with rN points in the generator, which consists of feature extraction, feature expansion, and coordinate reconstruction. The goal of the discriminator is to distinguish whether its input is produced by the generator.

the generator better able to perform the upsampling task. Specifically, for each input point cloud data $\mathcal{P}$, the goal of the generator is to produce dense and uniformly distributed point clouds $S = \left\{ s_i \in \mathbb{R}^{3 \times 1} \right\}_{i=1}^{rN}$, where p_i and s_i are the coordinates of 3D points, and r is the upsampling rate. The discriminator finds the fake data generated by the generator. Please see our previous work [4] for a detailed network structure.

2.3 Steps to Highlight the Soft Edges

Based on the ideas explained in Sects. 2.1 and 2.2, our proposed method to highlight the soft edges is formulated as follows.

STEP 1: Extract points that are assigned a feature value larger than a given minimal value, which defines the boundary of a soft-edge region. **STEP 2:** Execute the deep learning-based upsampling for the extracted edge points. **STEP 3:** Merge the original 3D-scanned points, which include points of the non-edge regions, with the upsampled edge points. **STEP 4:** Apply SPBR to the integrated point cloud to create an edge-highlighted transparent image of the target 3D-scanned point cloud.

3 Experiments

In this section, we show the visualization experiments of our method. We demonstrate that our deep learning-based upsampling network works well to highlight the soft edges of 3D-scanned point clouds based on the opacity-gradation effect.

3.1 Transparent Edge-Highlighting Visualization of Japanese Armor

Here, we show experimental results of applying our method to the Japanese armor with many soft edges. Figure 2 shows the visualization result for our 3D-scanned data of a Japanese armor helmet that contains many soft edges. Figure 2a shows the opaque point-based rendering without edge highlighting. Figure 2b shows the edge-highlighting transparent visualization by using the original opacity-based edge highlighting [1]. In Fig. 2b, the soft edges are visible as the opacity gradation areas, but the edge highlighting is not very clear (see the enlarged image in the rectangle). In the original opacity-based edge highlighting method, the opacity gradation is realized based on simple copying or duplication of edge points. Although this copying is recognizable as quasi-upsampling, many of the added points are rejected through point occlusion. Therefore, the edge-highlighting does not work well. Figure 2c shows the result of our method. The opacity gradation is realized based on our deep learning-based upsampling well. Since the added points are different from the original ones, the opacity gradation becomes more evident, not diminished by the point occlusion. Therefore, edge-highlighting becomes more effective than Fig. 2b (compare the enlarged images in the rectangles).

Figure 3 shows the visualization result for our 3D-scanned data of a Japanese armor suit, which has both soft and sharp edges. The point cloud has several sharp edges that appear as the horizontal lines at the jointing parts of rectangular plates. Besides, there are varieties of soft edges. Figure 3a shows the opaque point-based rendering without edge highlighting. Figure 3b shows the edge-highlighting transparent visualization by using

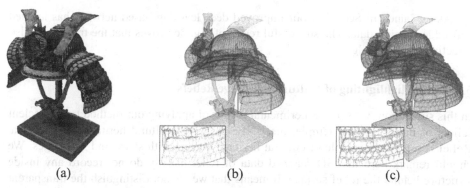

Fig. 2. Experimental results for 3D-scanned data of the Japanese armor helmet (10 million points). (a) shows the opaque point-based rendering without edge highlighting; (b) shows the transparent edge-highlighting visualization based on the original opacity-based edge highlighting [1]; (c) shows the transparent edge-highlighting visualization based on our method.

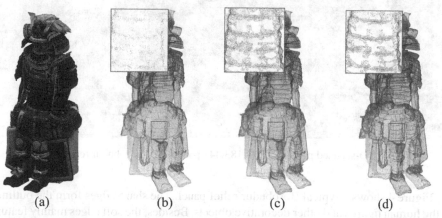

Fig. 3. Edge-highlighting visualization of the Japanese armor suite (10 million points). (a) shows the opaque point-based rendering without edge highlighting; (b) shows the edge-highlighting visualization based on the original opacity-based edge highlighting [1]; (c) shows the edge-highlighting visualization based on our method, and (d) shows the transparent edge highlighting visualization result of the upsampling network using the training set from our previous work.

the original opacity-based edge highlighting based on the point copying [1]. In Fig. 3b, the sharp edges are visible as thin horizontal lines but not very clear (see the enlarged image in the rectangle). Besides, the soft edges are not visible. Figure 3c shows the result of our method. We can observe the sharp edges clearer than Fig. 3b, and many soft edges are visible by the gradated colors (compare the enlarged images in the rectangles in Fig. 3b and Fig. 3c). Additionally, as shown in Fig. 3c and 3d, the result after adjusting the training set shows the soft-edge regions more clearly than the upsampling result obtained by using the training set in our previous work, and the generated new points are more clustered rather than diffused outside the edges.

As explained in Sect. 2.2, our improved deep learning-based network has learned soft-edge training data. The successful result of Fig. 3c proves that the training is also effective for sharp edges.

3.2 Edge Highlighting of Cultural Heritage Reliefs

In this subsection, we show experimental results of applying our method to the ancient reliefs of the Borobudur temple, the UNESCO world cultural heritage in Indonesia. Relief is a typical example of cultural heritage objects with sharp and soft edges. We should remark here that 3D scanned data of relief usually do not record any inside structure behind the relief surface. It means that we cannot distinguish the transparent visualization from opaque visualization. In such cases, our edge highlighting is available for photo-realistic edge-highlighting visualization.

Fig. 4. 3D-scanned point cloud (4,183,441 points) of a Borobudur relief panel.

Figure 4 shows a typical Borobudur relief panel. The sharp edges form the outlines of the human figures and other decorative objects. Besides, the soft edges mainly feature the details such as the tree branches and the human faces.

Figure 5a shows the edge-highlighting visualization of the data of Fig. 4 by using the original opacity-based edge highlighting based on the point copying [1]. Each drawn item is successfully characterized by the outlines expressed by the sharp edges. However, the details of each item are unclear because we cannot observe the soft edges clearly (see the enlarged image in the rectangle). Figure 5b shows the edge-highlighting result created by our method. The sharp edges are visualized clearly. Besides, we can observe the details with the help of the soft edges (compare the enlarged images in the rectangles in Fig. 5a and Fig. 5b).

Figure 6a shows the 3D-scanned point cloud of a famous Borobudur relief panel, where an ancient ship is drawn. The sharp edges express the outlines and the main structure of the ship. On the other hand, the soft edges should express the ocean waves (below the ship) and the clouds (upper right of the ship). Figure 6b shows the edge-highlighting by using the original opacity-based edge highlighting based on the point copying [1]. The sharp edges are visualized well, but the soft edges are not visualized clearly due to the insufficient local point density. The quasi-upsampling based on the

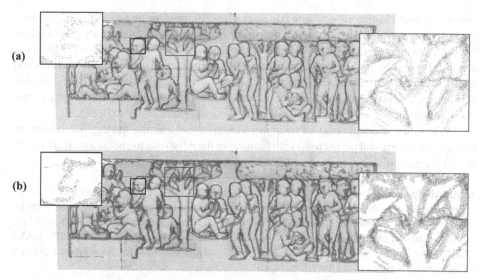

Fig. 5. Edge-highlighting visualization of the relief panel of Fig. 4. (**a**) shows the edge-highlighting visualization based on the original opacity-based edge highlighting [1]; (**b**) shows the edge-highlighting visualization based on our method.

point copying does not work well, especially around the soft edges. Figure 6c shows the edge-highlighting result created by our method. The soft-edge regions are given sufficient point density, and the soft edges are made clearly observable (compare the enlarged images in the rectangles in Fig. 6b and Fig. 6c).

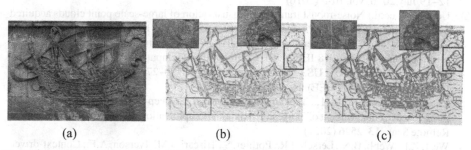

(a)	(b)	(c)

Fig. 6. Experimental results for 3D-scanned data of the Borobudur relief of the ancient ship (3,520,688 points). (**a**) shows the opaque point-based rendering without edge highlighting; (**b**) shows the edge-highlighting visualization based on the original opacity-based edge highlighting [1]; (**c**) shows the edge-highlighting visualization based on our method.

4   Conclusions

In this paper, we have proposed a robust edge-highlighting method applicable for 3D-scanned point clouds. By using our deep learning-based upsampling network, point density is made higher around the edge regions. The upsampling works well for both the soft and sharp edges. Applying the upsampling result to the opacity-based edge-highlighting makes the opacity gradation apparent. Then, the soft edges, which are usually difficult be highlighted, are successfully expressed. This feature of our method realizes comprehensible visualization of 3D scanned point clouds that record complex 3D shapes. We have demonstrated the effectiveness of our method by applying it to real 3D scanned data of cultural heritage objects.

In the future, we will consider adopting a multi-object training strategy that combines features of the original point cloud with features of the edge data to encourage the network to better distinguish between the edge and non-edge regions.

Acknowledgments. The authors would like to thank the Tokushima Castle Museum for its cooperation in executing the 3D scanning. The images of the Borobudur temple are presented with the permission of the Borobudur Conservation Office and Research Center for Area Studies (P2W) of the Indonesian Institute of Sciences (LIPI). This work is partially supported by JSPS KAK-ENHI Grant Numbers 19KK0256 and 21H04903, and the Program for Asia-Japan Research Development (Ritsumeikan University, Japan).

References

1. Kawakami, K., et al.: Opacity-based edge highlighting for transparent visualization of 3D scanned point clouds. ISPRS Ann. Photogramm. Remote. Sens. Spat. Inf. Sci. **5**, 373–380 (2020)
2. Tanaka, S., et al.: See-through imaging of laser-scanned 3D cultural heritage objects based on stochastic rendering of large-scale point clouds. In: Proceedings of the ISPRS Annals of Photogrammetry, Remote Sensing & Spatial Information Sciences, Prague, Czech Republic, 12–19 July 2016, vol. III-3 (2016)
3. Uchida, T., et al.: Noise-robust transparent visualization of large-scale point clouds acquired by laser scanning. ISPRS J. Photogramm. Remote. Sens. **161**, 124–134 (2020)
4. Yu, L., Li, X., Fu, C.-W., Cohen-Or, D., Heng, P.A.: PU-Net: point cloud upsampling network. In: Proceedings of the 2018 IEEE/CVF Conference on Computer Vision and Pattern Recognition, Salt Lake City, UT, USA, 18–23 June 2018, pp. 2790–2799. Institute of Electrical and Electronics Engineers (IEEE), New York (2018)
5. Li, W., Hasegawa, K., Li, L., Tsukamoto, A., Tanaka, S.: Deep learning-based point upsampling for edge enhancement of 3D-scanned data and its application to transparent visualization. Remote Sens. **13**, 2526 (2021)
6. West, K.F., Webb, B.N., Lersch, J.R., Pothier, S., Triscari, J.M., Iverson, A.E.: Context-driven automated target detection in 3D data. In: Proceedings of the Automatic Target Recognition XIV, Orlando, FL, USA, 21 September 2004 (2004)
7. Rusu, R.B.: Semantic 3D object maps for everyday manipulation in human living environments. KI Künstliche Intell. **24**, 345–348 (2010)
8. Weinmann, M., Jutzi, B., Mallet, C.: Semantic 3D scene interpretation: a framework combining optimal neighborhood size selection with relevant features. ISPRS Ann. Photogramm. Remote. Sens. Spat. Inf. Sci. **2**(3), 181–188 (2014)
9. Jutzi, B., Gross, H.: Nearest neighbour classification on laser point clouds to gain object structures from buildings. Int. Arch. Photogramm. Remote Sens. Spat. Inf. Sci. **38**, 4–7 (2009)
10. Corsini, M., Cignoni, P., Scopigno, R.: Efficient and flexible sampling with blue noise properties of triangular meshes. IEEE Trans. Vis. Comput. Graph. **18**, 914–924 (2012)

A Visual Analytics Method
for Time-Series Log Data Using Multiple
Dimensionality Reduction

Keijiro Fujita[1]($\boxtimes$), Naohisa Sakamoto[1] (iD), Takanori Fujiwara[2] (iD),
Jorji Nonaka[3] (iD), and Toshiyuki Tsukamoto[3] (iD)

[1] Kobe University, Rokko-dai, Nada, Kobe 657-8501, Japan
`216x223x@stu.kobe-u.ac.jp`
[2] University of California, Davis, One Shields Ave, Davis, CA 95616, USA
[3] RIKEN R-CCS, 7-1-26, Minatojima-minami, Chuo, Kobe, Japan

Abstract. The size and complexity of leading-edge high performance
computing (HPC) systems and their electrical and cooling facilities have
been continuously increasing over the years, following the increase in
both their computational power and heat generation. Operational data
analysis for monitoring the overall HPC system health and operational
behavior has become highly important for a reliable and stable long-
term operation as well as for operational optimizations. Operational log
data collected from the HPC system and its facility can be composed
by a wide range of information measured and sampled over time from
different kind of sensors, resulting multivariate time-series log data. In
our introduced visual analytics method, the HPC log data is represented
as third-order tensor (3D array) data with three axes corresponding to
time, space, and measured values. By applying multiple dimensionality
reduction steps, characteristic time and space can be identified and be
interactively selected for assisting the understanding of the HPC system
state and operational behavior.

Keywords: Visual analytics · Time-series · Log data · Dimensionality
reduction · High performance computing

1 Introduction

High performance computing (HPC) has become indispensable in various fields
of science and engineering for solving complex scientific problems and advancing
science and technology. Continuous demands for larger and faster computations
increase the overall size and performance of the HPC systems. For this purpose,
large-scale HPC systems, also known as supercomputers, have been developed
to perform high-performance computations through parallel processing using
multiple compute nodes that communicate with each other via high-bandwidth
interconnection network. To ensure continuous scheduling and execution of the
users' submitted HPC jobs, providing a reliable, stable HPC system operation
is highly important.

© Springer Nature Singapore Pte Ltd. 2022
B.-Y. Chang and C. Choi (Eds.): AsiaSim 2021, CCIS 1636, pp. 19–27, 2022.
https://doi.org/10.1007/978-981-19-6857-0_3

Modern HPC systems can collect various environmental data from a set of sensors to monitor the status of the hardware system and its supporting subsystems. These sets of data are usually stored periodically as log data, and can be often voluminous due to the scale and complexity of the HPC systems. The expansion of the number of monitoring components and the improvement of sensor technologies keeps further increasing the amount of collected data, including the increase in the measurement precision and the sampling rate. In order to effectively use the environmental log data, there is a growing demand for effective operational data analysis. However, due to its data size, it is not trivial to extract valuable information from the log data.

To address the above challenge of effective use of HPC log data, we introduce a visual analytics method, where we use dimensionality reduction (DR) methods multiple times. Through the multiple steps of DR, the method produces a 2D scatterplot from HPC log data that can be represented as a third-order tensor (or 3D array) with the axes of time, space, and measured values. This plot depicts the similarities of temporal points or spatial points based on an analyst's interest, and aids the analyst to find patterns, such as abnormal behaviors, from the vast amount of data. Additionally, to help understand the identified patterns from the scatterplot, we visualize the auxiliary information, including spatial information (e.g., the compute rack positions) and temporal information (e.g., the change of measured values). With interactive analysis using these visualizations, the analyst can effectively gain knowledge from HPC log data. We demonstrate the effectiveness of our visual analytics method through analyses of log data generated from the K computer.

2   Related Work

In order to efficiently analyze a large size of log data, various data analysis methods have been developed. As log data generated from HPC often has both temporal and spatial information, here we discuss visual analytics methods developed to review log data from temporal and/or spatial aspects. Xu et al. [9] developed a visual analysis tool, called ViDX, to help detect anomalies from assembly line log data. The tool can be used to hypothesize the causes of anomalies and their effects by focusing on temporal changes in the system efficiency. A few analysis tools are developed for HPC log data analysis, such as La VALSE [2] and MELA [7]. However, all the works above have limitations because they treat log data as a 2D array, and either the temporal or spatial features are required to be explicitly specified to determine the spatio-temporal region of interest.

Tensor decomposition methods have recently been attracting attention for the analysis of time-series data. Tensor decomposition is a method to decompose tensor data (or multidimensional array data) into a sum of smaller order tensors, including vectors and matrices, to reduce the dimensionality of data for extracting meaningful features. The CP (Canonical Polyadic) decomposition [4] and Tucker decomposition [8] are commonly used methods. For log data, Kimura

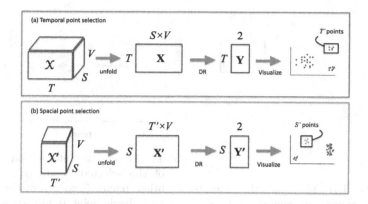

Fig. 1. An overview of the proposed method composed of (a) temporal point selection and (b) spacial point selection.

et al. [3] proposed a method to factorize log data represented as a tensor. However, the tensor decomposition results from these methods are usually not suitable for interactive analysis, without appropriate processing or reconstruction, since they only provide few clues to understand their intrinsic information.

On the other hand, instead of tensor decomposition, several researchers applied DR methods to tensor data to achieve more flexible analysis. For example, Fujiwara et al. [1] proposed a method to help interpret visualized clusters and outliers by interactively applying multiple rounds of DR through the stepwise selection of reference axes for third-order tensor data. However, for analyzing HPC log data, it becomes important to find not only the characteristic time or space but also the characteristic space-time, which is one of the most demanding requirements for HPC log analysis. In this work, we develop a method to find characteristic spatio-temporal features by applying multi-step DR to a given log data represented as third-order tensor data.

3 Methodology

An overview of our method is shown in Fig. 1. The method is designed to identify the spatio-temporal regions where the HPC system shows characteristic behaviors with the (a) time selection and (b) space selection interfaces.

3.1 Time Selection

From log data $\mathcal{X}$ ($\mathcal{X} \in \mathbb{R}^{T \times S \times V}$; T, S, V are the numbers of temporal points, spatial points, and measured values, respectively), which is represented as third-order tensor data, we apply DR to select temporal point clusters that show characteristic behavior of the HPC system. Since DR can only be applied to matrix data, it is necessary to expand and convert the third-order tensor data $\mathcal{X}$ to matrix data. To do so, as shown in Fig. 1(top), we slice $\mathcal{X}$ along the spatial

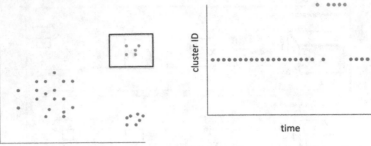

(a) The DR plot for the temporal points represented as Y. Red
points show a set of the user selected points.

(b) The temporal information plot
of the selected points (red) and
other points (gray) from the DR
plot. Each point is plotted along
the time axis for each point
group/cluster.

Fig. 2. Temporal point selection (Color figure online)

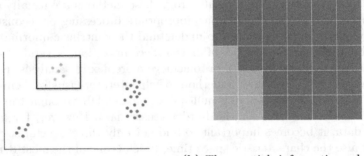

(a) The DR plot for spatial points represented as Y'. Blue points show
the set of selected points by the
user.

(b) The spatial information plot of
selected points (blue) and other
points (gray) in the DR plot. Each
point is represented as a square
and placed in a 2D plane according
to its spatial position.

Fig. 3. Spatial point selection (Color figure online)

axis and unfold into a matrix $\mathbf{X}$ with T rows and $S \times V$ columns. Then, by applying DR to this matrix $\mathbf{X}$, we can represent $\mathcal{X}$ as a matrix $\mathbf{Y}$ with T rows and
two columns. This matrix represents the time information of the time axis of log
data $\mathcal{X}$. Therefore, temporal points placed close to each other in the DR result
$\mathbf{Y}$ (e.g., red points highlighted in Fig. 1) can be expected to have similar behaviors. As DR methods through this paper, we use Principal Component Analysis
(PCA) [6] to compress the data and Uniform Manifold Approximation and Projection (UMAP) [5], which is a nonlinear DR method with low computational
overhead, to find similar points.

Next, we discuss how to visualize the DR result to select the temporal points of interest. The DR result $\mathbf{Y}$ can be plotted in a 2D space. However, it is difficult to automatically select clusters of interest from this plot (e.g., by using clustering algorithms) because the distances and arrangements of clusters can vary based on the DR algorithm. Thus, instead, we take an approach that allows the user to interactively select a cluster of interest. We first visualize the temporal points in $\mathbf{Y}$ as gray points. When interactively selecting a cluster, the selected temporal points are shown with a different color (e.g., red), as shown in Fig. 2a. Then, as shown in Fig. 2b, we visualize the temporal information of the points in each of the selected clusters (e.g., red and gray points in this case). From Fig. 2b, we can grasp the temporal distribution of the selected cluster. In addition to this temporal visualization, we compute the mean value of each measurement for each cluster (e.g., Table 2 in Sect. 5). By reviewing these mean values, we can understand which measures are most influential the differences between each cluster. With the pieces of information above (i.e., the DR result, the temporal distribution, and the mean values of measurements), our method allows the analyst to effectively find a temporal cluster of interest.

3.2 Space Selection

After the selection of T' temporal points of interest from all T points (Sect. 3.1), we extract $\mathcal{X}'$, the portion of log data, corresponding to the selected T' temporal points (refer to Fig. 1). Then, we follow a process similar to the time selection as shown in Fig. 1 and obtain $\mathbf{Y}'$ with S rows and 2 columns. This matrix $\mathbf{Y}'$ summarizes the spatial information of the partial log data $\mathcal{X}'$ in two dimensions/columns. We visualize the DR result as shown in Fig. 3a. Similar to the time selection, this DR result also allows to interactive selection of spatial points. The spatial information of each cluster (blue: selected, gray: non-selected) is visualized, as shown in Fig. 3b. This example shows the case where the HPC system has hardware devices (e.g., compute nodes) aligned on a plane and each spatial point corresponds one device representing as one square. After the time selection and spatial selection, we now identify the third-order tensor data with the size of $T' \times S' \times V$, which is considered to contain the user-interest, characteristic behavior of the HPC system.

4 Experimental Result

In order to verify the effectiveness of our method, we conduct an experiment using real HPC log data obtained from the K computer. We overview the behavior of the K computer and verify whether we can identify time and space where the K computer presented characteristic behaviors using the prototype system that implements the method we described in Sect. 3. To understand the trend of the behavior of the K computer per year, we analyze logs from April 2016 to March 2017.

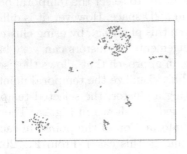

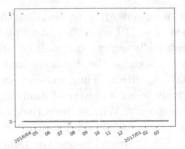

(a) The DR plot for temporal points

(b) The temporal information plot of selected points (red) and other points (gray).

Fig. 4. Results of the temporal point selection. (Color figure online)

Table 1. The mean values of measurements of the time point clusters.

	AirIn (°C)	AirOut (°C)	CPU (°C)	Water (°C)
Selected points	20.599	21.679	15.487	15.760
Others	21.199	25.346	17.814	15.962

The selected portion of log data is a daily average of four different temperature data measured every five minutes on each of 864 compute racks of the K computer for 361 days (from April 1, 2016 to March 31, 2017), excluding the four stopped days due to the scheduled maintenance period (from October 6 to October 9). Figure 4a shows the DR result of the log data for the time selection. Here, as we apply DR along both spatial points and measured values (i.e., $S \times V$ columns in Fig. 1(top)), the four temperature data from each of the 864 racks for one day are represented by a single time point. From Fig. 4a, we select a small cluster, which can be expected to have different patterns from the other majorities (i.e., potential abnormal behaviors). As shown in Fig. 4b, the selected time cluster is formed by the time points for eight days: (1) three days from April 2, 2016 to April 4, 2016, (2) July 8, 2016, (3) three days from October 10, 2016 to October 12, 2016, and (4) February 2, 2017. Table 1 shows the mean values of measured temperatures for the selected time cluster and the other time points. From Table 2, we can see the selected time cluster has substantially lower values for all the measured temperatures.

We then visualize the DR plot for spatial points (Fig. 5a) and select most of the spatial points, except for clear outliers (i.e., gray points located around the top-left corner). Figure 5b shows the spatial information of the compute racks. Table 2 shows the selected spatial cluster and the other spatial points. We can verify that the mean of each measured values (AirIn, AirOut, Average CPU temperature, and Cooling water temperature) are all low in the selected spatial cluster. We also notice that there are considerable differences in AirOut

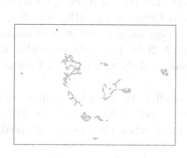

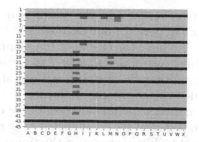

(b) The spatial information plot of selected points (blue) and other points (gray)

(a) The DR plot for spatial points

Fig. 5. Results of the spatial point selection (Color figure online)

Table 2. The mean values of measurements of the space point clusters.

	AirIn (°C)	AirOut (°C)	CPU (°C)	Water (°C)
Selected points	20.592	21.645	15.466	15.758
Others	20.997	23.574	16.642	15.873

and average CPU temperature between the selected cluster and the others when compared to the rest.

5 Discussion

We have conducted a practical experiment to demonstrate that our method can identify characteristic spatio-temporal features from environmental log data collected from an HPC system. From the experimental results, we have overviewed the behavior of the HPC system. Four measurements were all low in the selected time cluster, with AirOut and Average CPU temperature being particularly low. From this, it can be inferred that the compute node utilization was significantly low on the days corresponding to these time points. However, since the time points included in the selected time cluster are discontinuous, it is unlikely that the computational load on the selected spatial cluster was low for all included time points and high for the others. Since the mean temperature for the cluster of non-selected spatial points is lower than the overall average of AirOut measured in all compute racks, the compute racks corresponding to this cluster also have a low computational load in the overall view. Therefore, we can infer that the distribution of the selected spatial cluster was created by the fact that the selected time cluster included both the days when jobs were executed in any interval and the days when they were not executed at all. Thus, as an additional analysis, it is necessary to further divide the selected time cluster: the period from April 2, 2016 to April 4, 2016, which can be expected to have the effect of the system shutdown for the end-of-year maintenance from April 1, 2016 to April 5, 2016; the period from October 10, 2016 to October 12, 2016, which can be expected to have the effects of the planned power outage and system shutdown for maintenance from October 7 to October 12, 2016. From these results, it can be inferred that the system has been affected on July 8, 2016 and February 2, 2017 due to some external influence.

From these experimental results, we can confirm that our introduced method can comprehensively handle the temporal and spatial features of the HPC log data, and enables us to select the time and space when the system behaved in a characteristic way.

6 Conclusion

In this paper, we introduced a visual analysis method that enables us to efficiently select characteristic spatio-temporal features from log data obtained from HPC systems by using the third-order tensor expression and multiple dimensionality reduction. From the experimental evaluations, we show case that the introduced method can comprehensively handle the temporal and spatial features of the HPC system log data, and select the time and space where the system shows a characteristic behavior. In the future, we are planning to conduct additional experiments using log data from other HPC systems to verify the validity of the introduced method.

Acknowledgements. This work was partially supported by JSPS KAKENHI (Grand Number 20H04194)

References

1. Fujiwara, T., et al.: A visual analytics framework for reviewing multivariate time-series data with dimensionality reduction. IEEE Trans. Visual. ComputerGr. **27**(2), 1601–1611 (2021)
2. Guo, H., Di, S., Gupta, R., Peterka, T., Cappello, F.: La VALSE: scalable log visualization for fault characterization in supercomputers. In: Proceedings of EGPGV, pp. 91–100 (2018)
3. Kimura, T., et al.: Spatio-temporal factorization of log data for understanding network events. In: IEEE INFOCOM 2014-IEEE Conference on Computer Communications, pp. 610–618. IEEE (2014)
4. Kolda, T.G., Bader, B.W.: Tensor decompositions and applications. SIAM Rev. **51**(3), 455–500 (2009)
5. McInnes, L., Healy, J., Saul, N., Grossberger, L.: UMAP: uniform manifold approximation and projection. J. Open Source Softw. **3**(29), 861 (2018)
6. Pearson, K.: LIII. On lines and planes of closest fit to systems of points in space. The London, Edinburgh Dublin Philos. Mag. J. Sci. **2**(11), 559–572 (1901)
7. Shilpika, Lusch, B., Emani, M., Vishwanath, V., Papka, M.E., Ma, K.L.: MELA: a visual analytics tool for studying multifidelity HPC system logs. In: Proceedings of DAAC, pp. 13–18 (2019)

8. Tucker, L.R.: Some mathematical notes on three-mode factor analysis. Psychometrika **31**(3), 279–311 (1966)
9. Xu, P., Mei, H., Ren, L., Chen, W.: ViDX: visual diagnostics of assembly line performance in smart factories. IEEE Trans. Visual. Comput. Graph. **23**(1), 291–300 (2017)

Modeling and Simulation of Systems

Comparing the Conversion Effects of Toll Operations for Seoul Tollgate Using Arena

Seung-Min Noh[1] and Seong-Yong Jang[2(✉)]

[1] Korea Employment Information Service, Chungcheongbuk-do, Korea
[2] Seoul National University of Science and Technology, Seoul, Korea
syjang@seoultech.ac.kr

Abstract. Smart Tolling, which is believed to improve traffic flow when applied, was scheduled to be introduced in 2020 but has been delayed owing to labor issues. Instead of the Smart Tolling, Seoul Tollgate implemented Multi-Lane Hi-pass, which improved Hi-pass. The consequences of transitioning from the PAST model, which operated with toll collection system (TCS) and Hi-pass lanes, to the CURRENT model, which operated with Multi-Lane Hi-pass, TCS, and Hi-pass, were compared in this study, which referred to earlier research. In addition, the effects of switching from the CURRENT model to Smart Tolling were compared. The three toll operation models were implemented using Arena simulation software. Furthermore, 21 scenarios were designed to supplement the limitations of traffic simulation tools by expressing real-life conditions such as driver skills and weather conditions. Based on the time duration and level of congestion, the effect of conversion from the PAST to the CURRENT system was approximately 7.35% on average in the experiment. Converting from the CURRENT system to the Smart Tolling system can be estimated to enhance traffic throughput by approximately 24%.

Keywords: Arena simulation · Smart tolling · Multi-Lane Hi-pass · Tollgate

1 Introduction

Tollgate is one of the factors affecting smooth traffic flow on highways. Most tollgates currently use TCS lanes, which issue a ticket to a vehicle upon entering a highway, halt the vehicle at the exit, and collect tolls; and Hi-pass lanes, which allow vehicles to drive at speeds of less than 30 km/h and collect tolls [14, 27].

The smart highway project has been underway since 2007, with the goal of developing quick and safe intelligent highways that reduce traffic accidents and congestion [11, 13]. Smart Tolling, a technology that allows drivers to pay the tolls while traveling at their current speed, was developed [14]. Smart Tolling was supposed to be fully implemented in 2020, but it was delayed owing to concerns about job extinction caused by the preconditions of unmanned management [3].

The Ministry of Land, Infrastructure and Transport made efforts to improve the existing Hi-pass lane that has an excessively low speed limit of 30 km/h and a considerable

© Springer Nature Singapore Pte Ltd. 2022
B.-Y. Chang and C. Choi (Eds.): AsiaSim 2021, CCIS 1636, pp. 31–43, 2022.
https://doi.org/10.1007/978-981-19-6857-0_4

risk of collision owing to lane-widths of less than 3.5 m [20]. As a result, the Multi-Lane Hi-pass, which can be extended by connecting two or more Hi-Pass lanes and can reach a top speed of 80 km/h is being introduced across the country. On December 27, 2019, four existing Hi-pass lanes in the direction of the Seoul Tollgate exit, which serves as the spatial backdrop of the study, were converted into Multi-Lane Hi-pass lanes [21].

Noh et al. (2018) compared the effects of changing the Seoul Tollgate from TCS and Hi-pass lanes to Smart Tolling on traffic flow. Noh (2021) developed a simulator for Seoul Tollgate using Arena simulation software with visual basic for applications (VBA).

In this study, a new toll operation model with the Multi-Lane Hi-pass was added to the simulation model of Noh et al. (2018) to compare the conversion effects for the three toll operation systems. The toll operation models were implemented using Arena, which can handle continuous, discrete, and mixed situations [5], without VBA. Furthermore, the function was designed to supplement the restriction of traffic simulation tools such as PARAMICS and VISSIM in simulating the driver behavior by applying the driver competency and probability of lane shift for each driver. A reasonably realistic function, such as calculating speed factors based on weather conditions, was created.

2   Theory Background

2.1   Lane Types of Tollgates

The following are the types of tollgates: TCS that collects tolls with a ticket [8], Hi-pass that collects tolls by wirelessly communicating with the on-board unit (OBU) in the vehicle [7, 22], Multi-Lane Hi-pass that widens the lane of the Hi-pass and increases the speed limit [17], non-stop-based One Tolling that employs video recognition technology on private highways to collect tolls only at the last exit, without collecting interim tolls [19], and Smart Tolling that is a more advanced version of the Hi-pass with non-stop, multi-lane, high-speed toll collection [6, 17, 28]. Table 1 presents the comparison of the differences in lane types that have evolved with technological advancements [7, 17–19, 22].

2.2   Speed Factors Based on Weather Conditions

Unpredictable conditions, such as climate changes, are among the key causes of traffic congestion [2]. Rain, snow, and fog alter driving conditions and influence the driver behavior [12, 16]. However, light rain did not affect speed [29].

The content of the National Academies of Sciences, Engineering, and Medicine (2014) was the most plausible reference, as presented in Table 2, as a result of the structure of the material of the literature review [1, 4, 9, 10, 16, 23, 26].

Table 1. Characteristics by lanes.

Characteristic		Lane type			
		Hi-pass	Multi-lane hi-pass	One tolling	Smart tolling
Width		Narrow	Wide	Wide	Wide
Speed limit		≤30 km/h	50–80 km/h	Limit of highway	Limit of highway
Target		OBU vehicles	OBU vehicles	All vehicles	All vehicles
Recognition		Contact (sensor)	Contactless	Contactless	Contactless
Tolls	With OBU	Auto	Auto	Auto	Auto
	Without OBU	-	-	Only at the last exit	Deferred payment
Special note		Only OBU vehicles		On private highways	Without a ticket

Table 2. Speed factors based on weather conditions.

Weather condition	Rain (mm/h)		Snow (cm/h)			
	Medium (0.254–6.35)	Heavy (>6.35)	Light (≤0.127)	Light-medium (0.127–0.254)	Medium-heavy (0.255–1.27)	Heavy (>1.27)
Speed factor	0.93	0.92	0.87	0.86	0.84	0.83

2.3 Toll Operations

Table 3 shows how the tollgate operation was divided into three categories based on the lane types of tollgates and the number of actual operation lanes for Seoul Tollgate.

The first is the PAST method of operating 20 lanes, which includes TCS and Hi-pass.

The second is the CURRENT 18-lane operation method, which includes TCS, Hi-pass, and Multi-Lane Hi-pass.

The third option is Smart Tolling, which allows for passing without stopping while maintaining the five lanes open.

Table 3. Toll operations for Seoul Tollgate.

Operation model	Lane types and the number of lane by toll operations				Total number of lanes
	TCS	Hi-pass	Multi-lane hi-pass	Smart tolling	
PAST	13	7	-	-	20
CURRENT	11	3	4	-	18
Smart tolling	-	-	-	5	5

3   Simulation

This study referred the key assumptions for simulation and modeling by Noh et al. (2018) and Noh (2021).

3.1   Data

The Korea Expressway Corporation's actual traffic data (Monday, 3/21/2016), which had the highest traffic volume at the exit of the Seoul Tollgate at peak time (7 a.m. to 9 a.m.), were used by referring Noh et al. (2018). On the 20 lanes of the PAST model, 5, 6, 10, 14, and 20 lanes were not in use at that time, and the actual traffic volume was 12,481.

3.2   Assumptions

Arrival Distribution. The input analyzer included in Arena 14.0 was used to estimate the distribution of arrivals for the 15 lanes with traffic. For example, the estimation of the first lane suggested that the appropriate distribution is the exponential distribution, and the formula is 0.999 + EXPO (5.75) s. The results are listed in Table 4.

Table 4. Simulated and Observed traffic volumes (unit: s)

Lane number	Type	Arrival distribution	Traffic volume (vehicles)	
			Simulated	Observed
1	Hi-pass	0.999 + EXPO (5.75)	1,065.9 ± 10.61	1,066
2	Hi-pass	0.999 + EXPO (1.86)	2,513.87 ± 12.46	2,525
3	Hi-pass	0.999 + 26 × BETA (0.718, 4.85)	1,664.4 ± 12.86	1,671
4	Hi-pass	0.999 + EXPO (2.83)	1,873.33 ± 12.56	1,896
7	TCS	4 + GAMM (7.23, 2.23)	297.97 ± 4.34	293
8	TCS	7 + LOGN (15.7, 18.2)	324.37 ± 5.61	303
9	TCS	7 + LOGN (17.3, 22)	295.7 ± 4.8	285

(continued)

Table 4. (*continued*)

Lane number	Type	Arrival distribution	Traffic volume (vehicles)	
			Simulated	Observed
11	TCS	9 + EXPO (19.3)	260.4 ± 3.5	253
12	TCS	9 + EXPO (20.5)	241.8 ± 5	242
13	TCS	4 + EXPO (29.4)	218.4 ± 5.46	215
15	Hi-pass	0.999 + EXPO (4.85)	1,230.97 ± 11.26	1,230
16	Hi-pass	0.999 + EXPO (5.84)	1,051.33 ± 12.63	1,055
17	Hi-pass	0.999 + EXPO (6.26)	990.77 ± 9.84	993
18	TCS	8 + LOGN (27, 40.8)	210.4 ± 6.07	218
19	TCS	9 + GAMM (16.1, 1.25)	249.77 ± 2.97	236
Total			12,489.37 ± 24.95	12,481

Toll Collection Time. Assuming that the toll collection time (13 s) of the vehicles in the TCS lane is included in the arrival distribution.

Vehicle Type and Length. The traffic ratio for 6 vehicle types in each of the 15 lanes was confirmed by the Korea Expressway Corporation's public data portal[1]. For example, the first lane had 49% of Type 1, 0.6% of Type 2, 49.3% of Type 3, and 1.1% of Type 6. The assumed length based on the vehicle type was referenced to the design standards for tunnel ventilation in the Construction Digital Library[2], as shown in Table 5.

Table 5. Type and length of vehicles (unit: m)

	Type 1	Type 2	Type 3	Type 4	Type 5	Type 6
Class	Compact	Medium	Full-size (5.5–10 t)	Full-size (10–20 t)	Full-size (≥20 t)	Sub-compact
Length	4	5	8	9	14	4

Gap Distance. Because a driver prefers to maintain a gap from the vehicle ahead to avoid accidents, a gap of 1 m was assumed (see Fig. 1).

---

[1] Public data portal for Expressway Homepage: http://data.ex.co.kr.
[2] Construction Digital Library Homepage: https://www.codil.or.kr.

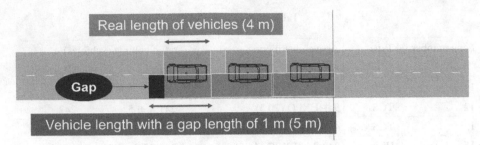

Fig. 1. Gap distance

Entry Road Section. The entry road was 368 m long from the tollbooth to the joining section, and it was split into 7 sections, as shown in Fig. 2.

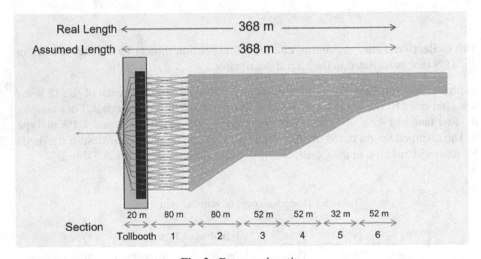

Fig. 2. Entry road section

Speed Limit by Section. To describe the deceleration for collecting tolls and the acceleration thereafter, there was restriction on the driving speed in certain sections, as shown in Table 6.

Occupy and Release Zones. When a vehicle moved ahead in an occupied zone, the current zone was released to let the next vehicle move ahead, similar to that in real life (see Fig. 3).

Driver Proficiency and Dynamic Movement. It was assumed that the vehicles that had to pay toll at the tollbooth move to the lane with the least number of vehicles. Novice drivers were chosen as being 10% of Type 1 and 30% of Type 6, and the probability of changing the lane was assumed to be 25%.

Table 6. Speed limit by section (units: km/h)

Section	Driving speed by lanes			
	TCS	Hi-pass	Multi-lane hi-pass	Smart tolling
Tollbooth	10 (stop 1 s)	30	MIN (user specified, 80)	User specified
1	User specified × 50%	User specified × 80%	User specified	User specified
2	User specified × 80%	User specified	User specified	User specified

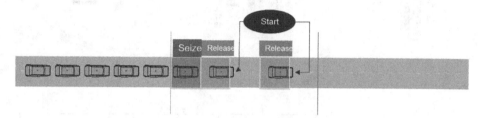

Fig. 3. Occupy and release zones

Mapping of the Lanes. The PAST, CURRENT, and Smart Tolling models have 20, 18, and 5 lanes respectively; therefore, the lanes must be mapped based on toll operations. The lane traffic volumes between the PAST and the CURRENT toll operation models were mapped equally. For the Smart Tolling model, an average of 2,496 vehicles per lane was mapped.

Figure 4 shows the lane mapping results between each model based on the PAST model.

3.3 Modeling

The simulation model was implemented using Arena 14.0 without VBA, and the model of Noh et al. (2018) was rebuilt in 4 phases. The sequence was:

First, send the vehicle that arrived at the tollgate to the appropriate lane based on the toll operation chosen during the experiment.

Second, assess the throughput time of the vehicle passing the tollbooth section.

Third, the situation of moving to the joining section by changing lanes.

Fourth, calculate the criteria when passing the end point of the final section.

Figure 5 demonstrates a run simulation for the CURRENT model with Multi-Lane Hi-pass.

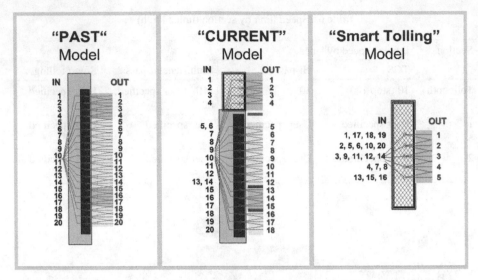

Fig. 4. Lane mapping results

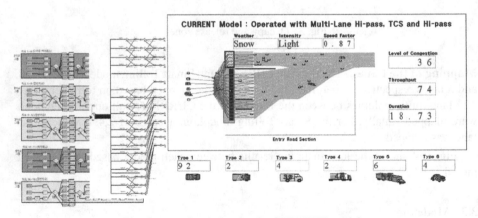

Fig. 5. Run simulation for the CURRENT model

3.4   Scenarios

When the Smart Tolling technology is used in the Seoul Tollgate, vehicles can drive at speeds of up to 110 km/h. Table 7 shows that scenarios were designed for weather conditions based on free flow.

Table 7. Scenario design

Weather	Intensity	Speed factor	Past	Current	Smart tolling
Clear	-	1	Sc1	Sc2	Sc3
Rain	Medium	0.93	Sc1-R1	Sc2-R1	Sc3-R1
	Heavy	0.92	Sc1-R2	Sc2-R2	Sc3-R2
Snow	Light	0.87	Sc1-S1	Sc2-S1	Sc3-S1
	Light-medium	0.86	Sc1-S2	Sc2-S2	Sc3-S2
	Medium-heavy	0.84	Sc1-S3	Sc2-S3	Sc3-S3
	Heavy	0.83	Sc1-S4	Sc2-S4	Sc3-S4

4 Experiment Results

4.1 Criteria

Because the new model was constructed according to the logic of Noh et al. (2018), the models must be compared using the same criteria. Table 8 presents the three criteria [24].

Table 8. Criteria to compare models

Criteria	Description
Level of congestion	The average number of vehicles in the entire section
Throughput	The level of traffic handling
Duration	The average time to go through the entire section

4.2 Number of Replications

Repeated experiments are necessary to statistically verify the validation of the results, because an experiment can be distorted by skewed patterns [15].

The simulation's replication time was set to 2 h, and the number of the replications was set to 30. The reliability of the results was verified based on the criteria. For all 21 scenarios, the 95% confidence level error rate in Sc2-R2 and Sc2-S4 was high but constant at 0.35% (see Table 9).

Table 9. 95% Confidence level error rate (units: %)

Scenario	Level of congestion	Throughput	Duration
Sc1	0.32	0.01	0.11
Sc1-R1	0.33	0.01	0.10
Sc1-R2	0.29	0.01	0.10
Sc1-S1	0.19	0.01	0.10
Sc1-S2	0.25	0.01	0.14
Sc1-S3	0.22	0.01	0.14
Sc1-S4	0.25	0.01	0.14
Sc2	0.34	0.01	0.11
Sc2-R1	0.32	0.01	0.16
Sc2-R2	0.35	0.01	0.16
Sc2-S1	0.30	0.01	0.10
Sc2-S2	0.23	0.02	0.15
Sc2-S3	0.26	0.02	0.10
Sc2-S4	0.35	0.02	0.15
Sc3	0.28	0,01	0
Sc3-R1	0.26	0.01	0
Sc3-R2	0.30	0.01	0
Sc3-S1	0.28	0.01	0
Sc3-S2	0.28	0.01	0
Sc3-S3	0.27	0.02	0
Sc3-S4	0.23	0.01	0

4.3   Results of the Simulation

Results by Criteria.   Table 10 summarizes the range of the experimental results for 21 scenarios based on the criteria grouped in toll operations.

Table 10. Simulation results

Model	Weather	Speed factor	Level of congestion	Throughput	Duration
PAST	Snow (Heavy)	0.83–1	28.6–32.22	99.72–99.77	18.66–21.9
CURRENT	- Clear		26.37–31.67	99.74–99.79	17.38–20.46
Smart Tolling			21.39–25.86	99.8–99.83	12.31–14.91

Key Results. In this study, the improvement using the Smart Tolling system over the CURRENT model was investigated.

The following are the outcomes:

First, the duration and the level of congestion decreased by 6.9% and 7.8%, respectively, when the CURRENT model was applied to the situation of the PAST model. As a result, the impact of the application was limited.

Second, the duration and the level of congestion decreased by 29.1% and 18.9%, respectively, when the Smart Tolling model was used indicating additional impacts. As a result, despite the comparison with the heavy snow scenario of the Smart Tolling model (Sc3-S4), which was based on the clear scenario of the CURRENT model (Sc2), the results of the Smart Tolling model were better (see Fig. 6).

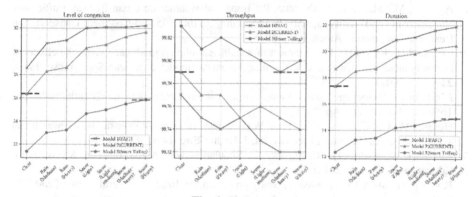

Fig. 6. Key results

5   Conclusion

The implementation of Smart Tolling has been delayed owing to the threat of job loss. In Seoul Tollgate, the Multi-Lane Hi-Pass was used instead of the Smart Tolling. In this study, the new model was developed by considering real-life characteristics such as driver skills and weather conditions. In addition, 21 scenarios were designed for three toll operations that included the CURRENT model, and a simulation was conducted to compare the effects of the conversion of the toll operation.

As a result, the conversion effect was compared based on the duration and level of congestion because the throughput was not significant. The conversion effect from the PAST to the CURRENT model was only 7.35% on average. Furthermore, traffic flow could be improved by an average of 24% by applying the Smart Tolling model.

Smart Tolling can be implemented at all tollgates, including the Seoul Tollgate, by resolving the issue of employment loss through the efforts of the government, resulting in improved traffic flow.

The following are the limitations:

The true impacts of speed factors may vary because the speed factors for each weather condition are not intended for tollgates. However, the function that changes this factor is significant for traffic simulation.

The front and rear sections, adjoining the spatial background of this study, were not included in the simulation. As a result, the simulations were conducted assuming traffic with no queueing.

Future work will necessitate the expansion to nearby tollgates and the flexibility to function in various scenarios.

Acknowledgement. This study was supported by the Research Program funded by the Seoul National University of Science and Technology.

References

1. Agarwal, M., Maze, T., Souleyrette, R.: Impact of weather on urban freeway traffic flow characteristics and facility capacity. In: Proceedings of the 2005 Mid-Continent Transportation Research Symposium, Ames, Iowa (2005)
2. Cheon, S.H., Rho, J.H.: Development of a traffic simulation model analyzing the effects of highway incidents using the CA (Cellular Automata) model. J. Korean Soc. Transp. **19**(6), 219–227 (2001)
3. Digitaltimes Homepage. http://www.dt.co.kr/contents.html?article_no=201806250210103 1650001. Accessed 03 Apr 2021
4. Hong, S.M., Oh, C., Yang, C.H., Jeon, W.H.: Effects of snowfall intensity on freeway travel speed: focused on Seohaean Freeway. Int. J. Highw. Eng. **14**(4), 93–101 (2012)
5. Kelton, D.W., Sadowski, R., Zupick, N.: Simulation with Arena, 6th edn. McGraw-Hill Education, New York (2014)
6. Korea Expressway Corporation: A Study on commercialization and evaluation of SMART Tolling system in case of more than 4 lanes, Korea Expressway Corporation (2017)
7. Korea Expressway Corporation: A Study on the Policy of Expressway Tolls. Korea Expressway Corporation (2010)
8. Korea Expressway Corporation: Road Design Guidelines Vol. 1: Road Planning and Geometry. Korea Expressway Corporation (2020)
9. Korea Institute of Construction Technology, Korea Transport Institute: Final Report on revision and supplementation of the Road Capacity Manual (Second year). Ministry of Land, Transport and Maritime Affairs (2011)
10. Korea Transport Institute: Methodology for the Estimation of Non-Recurrent Traffic Congestion Costs. Korea Transport Institute (2009)
11. Korea Transport Institute: Research for Traffic Model Revision Affected by ITS Operation: Case Study on Road Capacity Improvement. Korea Transport Institute (2013)
12. Kwak, H.Y., Joh, C.H.: A study on the impact of rainfall and traffic volume on traffic accidents: a case of Donghae and Yeongdong Expressways. J. Clim. Res. **10**(3), 263–272 (2015)
13. Lee, S.W., Oh, H.S.: Communication technology of smart highway. Inf. Commun. Mag. **27**(11), 28–35 (2010)
14. Lee, U.J., Kim, S.T., Kim, C.G., Park, J.H., Park, G.H.: Next generation tolling system with multi-lane and non-stop (SMART Tolling). Korean Soc. Road Eng. **16**(1), 46–50 (2014)
15. Rossetti, M.D.: Simulation Modeling and Arena, 1st edn. Wiley, Hoboken (2009)
16. Maze, T.H., Agarwal, M., Burchett, G.: Whether weather matters to traffic demand, traffic safety, and traffic operations and flow. J. Transp. Res. Board **1948**(1), 170–176 (2006)
17. Ministry of Land, Infrastructure and Transport Homepage. https://www.molit.go.kr/USR/NEWS/m_71/dtl.jsp?id=95078761. Accessed 20 May 2021

18. Ministry of Land, Infrastructure and Transport Homepage. https://www.molit.go.kr/USR/NEWS/m_71/dtl.jsp?id=95083677. Accessed 21 Feb 2021
19. Ministry of Land, Infrastructure and Transport Homepage. https://www.molit.go.kr/USR/NEWS/m_71/dtl.jsp?lcmspage=1&id=95073893. Accessed 06 Feb 2021
20. Ministry of Land, Infrastructure and Transport Homepage. https://www.molit.go.kr/USR/NEWS/m_72/dtl.jsp?id=95083240. Accessed 07 Mar 2021
21. Ministry of Land, Infrastructure and Transport: Implementation plan for intelligent transportation system in 2020. South Korea (2020)
22. Ministry of Land, Infrastructure and Transport: Roadway manual. South Korea (2020)
23. National Academies of Sciences, Engineering, and Medicine: Incorporating travel time reliability into the highway capacity manual. The National Academies Press, Washington, DC (2014)
24. Noh, S.-M., Kang, H.-S., Jang, S.-Y.: Improving traffic flow at a highway tollgate with ARENA: focusing on the Seoul Tollgate. In: Li, L., Hasegawa, K., Tanaka, S. (eds.) AsiaSim 2018. CCIS, vol. 946, pp. 501–510. Springer, Singapore (2018). https://doi.org/10.1007/978-981-13-2853-4_39
25. Noh, S.M.: A study on the design and development of the Smart Tolling simulator at the Seoul Tollgate using ARENA. Ph.D. dissertation, Seoul National University of Science and Technology, Seoul, South Korea (2021)
26. Prevedouros, P.D., Kongsil, P.: Synthesis of the effects of wet conditions on highway speed and capacity. University of Hawaii at Manoa, Honolulu. Hawaii (2003)
27. Sin, H.G., Nam, D.H.: Optimum speed simulation for electronic toll collection. J. Inst. Internet Broadcast. Commun. 13(3), 87–92 (2013)
28. Song, S.G., Ham, E.H., Jin, J.H., Go, M.G., Baek, H.S.: Analysis of the improvement effect to free-flow tolling system on expressway. Transp. Technol. Policy 13(4), 51–56 (2016)
29. Transportation Research Board: Highway capacity manual. Transportation Research Board, Washington, DC (2000)

CollabOffloading: A Computational Offloading Methodology Using External Clouds for Limited Private On-Site Edge Servers

Junhee Lee[1,2], Jaeho Jeon[1], and Sungjoo Kang[1(✉)]

[1] Electronics and Telecommunications Research Institute (ETRI), Daejeon, Republic of Korea
{j.h.lee,jeonjaeho11,sjkang}@etri.re.kr
[2] Korea Advanced Institute of Science and Technology (KAIST) , Daejeon, Republic of Korea
the78910@kaist.ac.kr

Abstract. In this paper, we proposed a methodology using Kubernetes clustered on-site edge servers with external clouds to provide computational offloading functionality for resource-limited private edge servers. This methodology enables additional functionalities without changing hardware infrastructures for industrial areas such as manufacturing systems. We devised a compute-intensive task scheduling algorithm using real-time CPU usage information of Kubernetes cluster to determine computation offloading decision. The purpose of the experiment is to compare overall performance between on-site edge only cluster and external cloud offloading cluster. The experiment scenario contains complex simulation problem which selects optimal tollgate for congested traffic situation. The result of experiment shows the proposed CollabOffloading methodology reduces entire execution time of simulations.

Keywords: Edge computing · Cloud computing · Kubernetes · Computation offloading · Scheduler · Simulation

1 Introduction

Recently smart sensors, Internet of Things (IoT), and advanced cellular network technologies such as 5G/6G has enabled private industrial on-site edge computing environment [1]. Private industrial on-site edge refers to the role of edge computing in industries such as manufacturing, oil and gas, and mining. The edge server is a system that provides a way for people to interact with the system in the industrial field by providing various features based on the connectivity between facilities, machines, and production environments in the private on-site environment. New advanced features such as digital twin, predictive maintenance, and remote operation are now being deployed to industrial sites through the edge servers.

Especially, Autonomous Things (AuT) such as industrial robot, drones, autonomous self-manufacturing facilities, which are capable of collecting and analyzing real-time data to solve problems like autonomous decision making for individual or collaborative

© Springer Nature Singapore Pte Ltd. 2022
B.-Y. Chang and C. Choi (Eds.): AsiaSim 2021, CCIS 1636, pp. 44–55, 2022.
https://doi.org/10.1007/978-981-19-6857-0_5

swarms of AuT devices [2]. The mentioned problems require high-performance computing (HPC) and compute-intensive capabilities such as computer simulations. However
industrial devices mainly have inferior computing capabilities, it is difficult to execute
compute-intensive jobs. Furthermore, because basic assumption of behaviors among
multiple AuTs or IoTs devices is to interact with each other, large scale of real-time
simulation is difficult for the device without external computing capabilities.

The concept of Computing Continuum has emerged, which assumes cyberinfrastruc-
ture surrounds the real-world environments. It enables AuTs to use HPC using Cloud
infrastructure as a service when necessary. The edge computing environment is a special
case of near-field infrastructure to obtain low latency computing results, and it can be
constructed by multi-access edge computing (MEC) or private on-site network.

Edge computing technology is appropriate for time critical compute-intensive jobs
rather than using devices' native computing resources. However, edge computing is different from Cloud computing that edge has limited resources while Cloud has almost
infinite resources [4]. Therefore, balanced scheduling methodology among edge computing and Cloud computing is required to properly provide time critical and compute
intensive tasks for AuTs.

There are relevant researches using edge and Cloud computing to support simulations. Balouek-Thomert et al. [5] conducted a research for scheduling and managing
heterogeneous resources using edge and Cloud, but because it is based on historical
data (e.g. minimization of WAN traffic, cost, and energy), it is not suitable for real-time
situation. Peltonen et al. [6] suggested edge and Cloud computing continuum environment for vehicles, but their experiments are limited in edge and Cloud environment, and
collaboration between heterogeneous Clouds and edges are not considered.

In this paper, we propose a CollabOffloading methodology which is a collaborated
computing platform consisted of edge and heterogeneous Clouds to provide computation
offloading for devices. It considers real-time edge resources and when edges have insufficient CPU resources, it dynamically switches to the tasks to the heterogeneous Clouds.
To evaluate the platform, we used four on-premise edge servers and two commercial
external clouds and executed the scenario of tollgate selecting simulation [3].

2   Background

2.1   Kubernetes

Kubernetes is an open-source container orchestration engine for automating deployment,
scaling, and management of containerized applications [7]. Initially, Kubernetes was
developed by Google, but now Cloud Native Computing Foundation manages Kubernetes. Kubernetes connects multiple nodes (servers) and constructs a cluster, and orches-
trates workloads among the servers. Kubernetes servers are consisted of control-plane
node and worker node. The control-plane node manages the whole cluster. And it contains
kube-apiserver, kube-controller-manager, kube-scheduler, and etcd. In the Kubernetes,
the Pods are the smallest deployable units of computing that users can create and manage
in Kubernetes [7], and it may contain one or more containers. Generally, normal Pods
are not deployed to control-plane node because overhead on the control-plane node may
cause instability of cluster. The normal Pods are deployed to worker nodes which are
mainly concentrating on running applications.

2.1.1 Kubernetes Scheduling Framework

The kube-scheduler in the control-plane node schedules and decides where the Pods are deployed. It has a scheduling framework which has several extension points for providing lightweight and flexible maintenance functionality [8]. The scheduling framework of Kubernetes is described in Fig. 1. The plugins can be applied to each extension points. The applied plugins affect their functions at certain stage of extension point during scheduling. The scheduling framework has scheduling cycle and binding cycle. In the scheduling cycle, it decides which node is most suitable to deploy Pod. Then Kubernetes binds the Pod to the selected node in binding cycle. There are several default plugins already applied to each extension points, such as ImageLocality and TaintToleration.

As described in Fig. 1, scheduling cycle is consisted of eight extension points. Among the extension points, similar things can be categorized as filtering, and scoring phase. There are three extension points in filtering phase: PreFilter, Filter, and PostFilter. In filtering phase, it excludes unqualified nodes for the Pod. For example, if some application requires GPU hardware, it must be deployed to the node that includes GPU. Therefore, the developer registers GPU requirement information to 'NodeAffinity' attribute of the Pod before deploying. Because the default plugin 'NodeAffinity' is already installed at the Filter extension point, it filters nodes that have no GPU hardware.

In scoring phase, scheduler gives scores on the filtered nodes to decide which node will be the best one to deploy the Pod. There are three extension points in scoring phase: PreScore, Score, and Normalize Score. If there are several plugins at the Score extension point, it adds calculated scores from each plugin. The 'NodeResourcesLeastAllocated' is the default score plugin in Score extension point, which gives higher score for the least resource allocated nodes. The node with relatively less allocated resources tends to be scheduled for Pod deployment. The Normalize Score extension point normalizes the cumulated scores which makes the highest score of 100. After the scoring phase, the node for Pod is selected and it binds to the node during the binding cycle.

2.1.2 Kubernetes Taints and Tolerations

Kubernetes Taints make restrictions to nodes that under certain conditions, they cannot deploy Pods. Kubernetes Tolerations are assigned to Pods, and the tolerated Pod can be deployed to the tainted node. In other words, Pod Tolerations override node Taints. The Taints have three effects: NoSchedule, PreferNoSchedule, NoExecute. Kubernetes scheduler never schedules to NoSchedule tainted node. PreferNoSchedule Taint is a soft version of NoSchedule that Kubernetes scheduler tries not to schedule to PreferNoSchedule tainted node. NoExecute Taint is the most forceful one that NoExecute tainted node evicts all running Pods except tolerated Pods, and Kubernetes scheduler never schedules to NoExecute tainted node. Kubernetes Tolerations are defined in Pod's pod.spec.toleration. It has key, operator, value, and effect as sub properties. The operator has two types: Exists and Equal. When the operator is Exists, even if 'key' and 'effect' (except 'value') are matched between Taint and Toleration, it regards as suitable Toleration. On the other hand, when the operator is Equal, 'key', 'effect', and 'value' must be matched for valid Toleration.

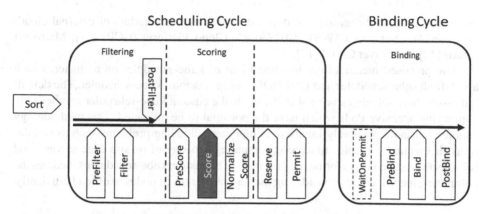

Fig. 1. Scheduling framework of Kubernetes [9]

The example of Taints and Tolerations is described in Fig. 2. Figure 2 line 1 shows how to assign Taint to node, and line 2 shows how to delete Taint from the node. Figure 2 line 3 shows how to assign Toleration for key1 Taint. If a Pod contains this Toleration, it can be scheduled NoSchedule tainted node1.

```
1. Assign NoSchedule Taint to node1
$ kubectl taint node node1 key1=value1:NoSchedule

2. Delete NoSchedule Taint from node1
$ kubectl taint node node1 key1=value1:NoSchedule-

3. Toleration for key1 Taint
tolerations:
- key: "key1"
  operator: "Equal"
  value: "value1"
  effect: "NoSchedule"
```

Fig. 2. Example of taints and toleration

3   CollabOffloading Methodology

3.1   Structure of CollabOffloading Methodology

The number of on-site edge nodes is fixed because it supposes an industrial site such as resource-limited inferior manufacturing sites. Figure 3 shows the proposed structure of CollabOffloading methodology. The on-site edge Kubernetes cluster is consisted of four nodes (one control-plane node and three worker nodes). Then cloud-based external Kubernetes worker nodes are connected to the constructed Kubernetes cluster. For failure safety and availability reason, we decided to diversify the vendors of external cloud; Amazon Web Services (AWS) [10], Google Cloud Platform (GCP) [11], Microsoft Azure [12], and Naver Cloud [13].

The proposed methodology has two kinds of kube-scheduler on a cluster, which are default kube-scheduler and CollabOffloading (custom) kube-scheduler. The default kube-scheduler schedules normal Pods, while the custom kube-scheduler handles only computing intensive Pods which have the potential to be offloaded. This methodology enables to handle massively intensive computing offloading problems such as simulations. It eventually enables to exceed computing capacity of on-site edge servers, and refrains to degrade the performance of servers. The custom kube-scheduler schedules the computing intensive Pods considering the resource status of nodes to offload efficiently.

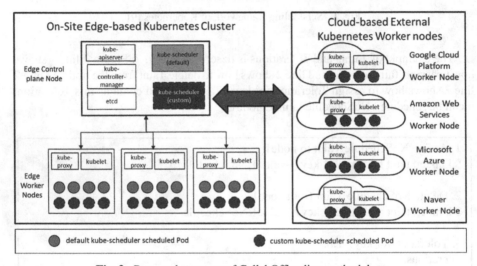

Fig. 3. Proposed structure of CollabOffloading methodology

3.2   Design of CollabOffloading Kube-Scheduler

The basic policy of the Kubernetes scheduler's default plugins does not consider current node resources. The default scoring plugin, 'NodeResourcesLeastAllocated', evaluates the score using requested information determined by the Pod deployer rather than the resource state. Additional installation of Kubernetes metric server can collect real-time resource usage information of edge nodes. The Kubernetes metric server fills data to v1beta1.MetricsV1beta1Interface, and Kubernetes API server provides the API which allows applications to access the resource information. We figured out that load metric information function is extremely time-consuming process that it consumes nearly 200ms per a function call. Therefore, we divided this metric information collecting task as an extra thread that cannot be affected to performance of scheduling process. Consequently, the overall performance of CollabOffloading kube-scheduler became same as the default kube-scheduler.

We devised an Algorithm that decides the offloading situation, which is described as Algorithm 1. When offloading is required, Algorithm 1 assigns a Kubernetes toleration to the Pod to be offloaded. The Algorithm 1 has two parameters as an input: (1) set of node N, which contains φ(CPU Capacity), χ(CPU Usage), ψ(Node Label Key), ω(Node Label Value) as member variables, (2) threshold ratio of CPU τ. The criterion of offloading decision is current CPU usage ratio (CPURatio) of on-site edge nodes. Which means cloud-based external worker nodes are not considered as described in line number 5 of the Algorithm 1. When every on-site edge nodes' CPU usage exceeds a threshold ratio of CPU τ, the Pod offloading process begins. After Pod offloading is decided, the Algorithm assigns NoSchedule toleration for 'node.kubernetes.io/unschedulable' to the Pod. Then the Pod can be scheduled on NoSchedule tainted nodes, which is known as cloud nodes in this context.

Algorithm 1: Decide Pod offloading and assign Pod tolerance

Parameters:
$\{\varphi$(CPU Capacity)$, \chi$(CPU Usage)$, \psi$(Node Label Key)$, \omega$(Node Label Value)$\} \in$ N(Set of Nodes)$, \tau$(Threshold ratio of CPU)

      INITIALIZATION:
1:   **set** isOffload $\leftarrow$ *true*
2:   **set** CPURatio $\leftarrow$ 0
3:   **set** Toleration $\leftarrow$ $\{null, null, null\}$
      OFFLOADING DECISION:
4:   **for** $i = 1$ **to** $|N|$ **do**
5:     **if** $N_{i.\psi} = $ "$location$" $\wedge$ $N_{i.\omega} = $ "$cloud$" **then**
6:       **continue**
7:     **end if**
8:     **set** CPURatio $\leftarrow$ $N_{i.\chi}$ / $N_{i.\varphi}$
9:     **if** CPURatio $< \tau$ **then**
10:     **set** isOffload $\leftarrow$ *false*
11:      **break**
12:     **end if**
13:   **end for**
      OFFLOADING ASSIGN:
14:   **if** isOffload = *true*
15:     **set** Toleration $\leftarrow$ $\{$"*node.kubernetes.io/unschedulable*", "*Exists*", "*NoSchedule*"$\}$
16:   **end if**
      FINALIZATION:
17:   **return** Toleration

---

4 Experiments

4.1 Experiment Design

Because the CollabOffloading methodology is designed for industry field such as manufacturing sites which may have resource limitation problems, there are four on-site edge nodes to represent limited resource. We considered AWS, GCP, Azure, and Naver as external cloud nodes to connect on the cluster which described in Fig. 3. However, the technical issue of Azure and Naver cloud leads to AWS and GCP as the only two external clouds that can be connected on the Kubernetes cluster. Kubernetes Pod to Pod communication using calico container network interface (CNI) plugin [14] requires IPv4 encapsulation protocol, while Azure and Naver's firewall policy does not support the IPv4 protocol. Therefore, different from the initial plan, final structure for experiment became four on-site edge nodes and two external cloud nodes; AWS and GCP. The specifications of nodes are described in Table 1. The reason why number of CPU cores differ within the cloud nodes is because GCP cloud restricts the number of CPU cores less than 24 in a particular region. The original intention was 32 cores for each cloud nodes with same performance specification, but the cloud vendors' policies were different from others.

Table 1. Experiments environment

Nodes	CPU	Memory	OS	Kubernetes version
Control-plane Edge Node	Intel i7-9800X 3.8 GHz 16cores	128 GB	Ubuntu 20.04	v1.21.1
Edge Worker Node 1	Intel i7-9800X 3.8 GHz 16cores	128 GB		
Edge Worker Node 2	Intel i7-9800X 3.8 GHz 16cores	128 GB		
Edge Worker Node 3	Intel i7-9800X 3.8 GHz 16cores	128 GB		
AWS Cloud Worker Node	AMD EPYC 7R32 3.3 GHz 32cores	64 GB	Ubuntu 18.04	
GCP Cloud Worker Node	Intel Xeon 2 GHz 24cores	64 GB		

4.2 Case Study: Tollgate Selection Simulation Scenario

The case study scenario deals with a tollgate selection problem [3]. When a vehicle is entering the toll collection system (tollgate) on highway, the vehicle requests which gate is the shortest path to the edge computing platform, then the platform simulates based on the nearby traffic situation. Because actions of other vehicles are stochastic, compute intensive repeated simulation increases the probability of simulation result. Generally, computing resource is highly limited in every vehicle, so simulation request becomes computation offloading request. We thought this problem is similar as industrial problem such as management simulation at distribution center of the manufacturing site.

The detailed explanation of tollgate selection scenario begins. The main purpose of the case study is to maximize the utilization by providing the optimal tollgate information to the vehicles for congested tollgate situation. In other words, waiting time of each vehicle must be minimized. Figure 4(a) depicts the scenario graphically. The tollgate is consisted of two kinds of types: the Electronic Toll Collection System (ETCS) which is an automatic toll collection system, and the Toll Collection System (TCS) which is operated by human. The type of vehicles is manually driven vehicle (MDV) and autonomous vehicle (AV). The main rule of vehicles as follows: MDVs go to either ETCS or TCS, while AVs must go to ETCS. Because MDV is handled by human, where sometimes people do not follow what navigation says, MDV stochastically does not follow the direction from simulation result in order to reflect real-world situation. Also, exit direction after passing the tollgate is important consideration because sudden line change may cause traffic accident.

Figure 4(b) represents the structure of simulation model of this scenario. There are one transducer, one generator, five buffers, and five processor models. Every buffer model is connected to the Processor models and the buffers are regarded as a waiting line of the tollgate. The location of Buffer1 and Processor1 is assumed as left side, Buffer5 and Processor5 is assumed as right side. The generator model generates vehicles according to Poisson distribution with randomly assigned attributes (driver type, exit direction). The generated vehicle is moved to the selected buffer decided by optimal buffer selection algorithm and waits its order until linked processor finishes its task. The buffer is first-in-first-out (FIFO) queue. The Transducer model collects the information of processed vehicles and generates statistical results. Because the scenario contains stochastic variables such as random vehicle generation, the more simulations leads to higher accuracy, which is called Monte-Carlo simulation [15]. To execute the Monte-Carlo simulation, the higher repetition number of simulations is a computationally intensive resource-consuming task. Because the industrial manufacturing field has limited resources and due to lack of infrastructure environment, massive simulation cannot be conducted. The proposed CollabOffloading enables the simulation tasks using offloading functionality.

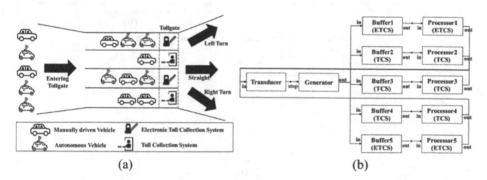

(a)   (b)

Fig. 4. Tollgate selection scenario (b) structure of simulation models [3]

4.3 Experiment Performance Evaluation

The purpose of this experiment performance evaluation is to compare on-site edge only execution and CollabOffloading method with external clouds. Based on the scenario described in Sect. 4.2, we set 10,000 vehicles generated per one simulation. To increase the accuracy of simulation result, repetitive simulations are executed. The terminology of this experiment: simulation request from client device is 'Offloading Request', the number of repetitive simulations per one offloading request is 'Simulation Counts per Request', and the interval time between requests is 'Time Interval'.

The experiment 1 is shown in Fig. 5(a). The fixed variables are follows: the time interval between requests is 1 s, the total offloading request is 100. With these fixed variables, simulation counts per request is between 500 and 3,000, increased by 500. The experiment 2 is shown in Fig. 5(b). The fixed variables are follows: the time interval between requests is 0.5 s, the total offloading request is 100. With these fixed variables, simulation counts per request is between 500 and 3,000, increased by 500. The difference between experiment 1 and experiment 2 is the time interval. In the experiment 1 and 2, we figured out the overall execution time of CollabOffloading is less than On-Site Edge only, and the shorter time interval makes the longer execution time. CollabOffloading uses the Kubernetes metric server, which scraps system resource every 15 s. Consequently, it becomes the limitation of CollabOffloading methodology because it cannot reflect real-time resources appropriately during the scheduling. In other words, Pods are scheduled to on-site edge nodes rather than cloud nodes. Therefore, additional experiment is required to measure the average tendency of the execution time as the offloading request increases.

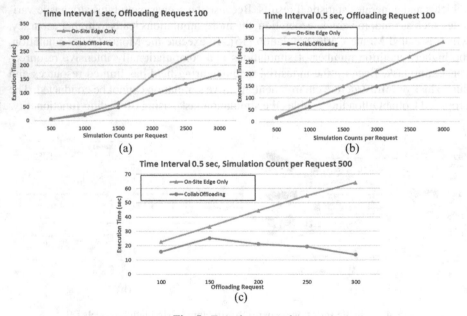

Fig. 5. Experiment results

The experiment 3 is shown in Fig. 5(c). The fixed variables are follows: the time interval between requests is 0.5 s, the simulation count per request is 500. With these fixed variables, offloading request is between 100 and 300, increased by 50. As a result of the experiment, when offloading request increased, the execution time of CollabOffloading decreased. It represents that appropriately scheduled Pods, deployed to the external cloud nodes, improves performance of the experiment. Therefore, we expect if the scrapping interval decreases, the overall performance of CollabOffloading will increase.

4.4 Graphical User Interface (GUI) for CollabOffloading Platform

We developed web-based graphical user interface which improves visual awareness of Pod offloading with a modified version of kube-ops-view [16]. It is depicted as in Fig. 6. It divides edge nodes to the left side and cloud nodes to the right side. The default scheduled Pod is represented as a rectangle, and the custom scheduled Pod is represented as a circle. The normal state of edge node is in yellow, while load exceeds over 80% of capacity, it turns to red. Figure 6(a) is the default state of cluster. As tasks are requested, Fig. 6(b) shows two of edge nodes turned to red, indicating that their tasks exceeded load capacity. Figure 6(c) shows all of edge node turned to red and that is the point where some Pods are deployed to cloud nodes. Figure 6(d) shows when the state of edge nodes turns back to its normal state, Pods are deployed to yellow edge nodes again.

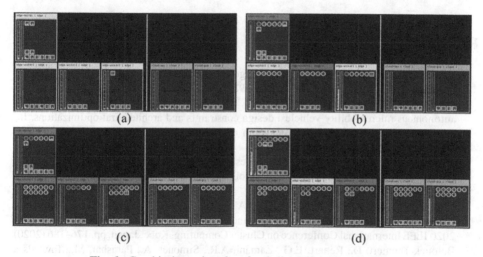

Fig. 6. Graphical user interface for CollabOffloading platform

5   Conclusion

New devices such as industrial robots, drones, and autonomous systems are appearing in industrial fields. They will make the industrial site itself more intelligent through new features such as artificial intelligent, digital twin, and predictive maintenance. However, in order for these AuTs to make autonomous decisions in unpredictable situations, high performance server systems or cloud computing infrastructures are required.

In this paper, we proposed CollabOffloading methodology for private industrial on-site edge servers to provide compute-intensive, high-performance computing capabilities such as simulations. This methodology enables additional functionalities without changing hardware infrastructures for industrial areas such as manufacturing systems.

The CollabOffloading Kubernetes scheduling algorithm considers real-time CPU usage and determines which node is the best one for to be scheduled Pod.

We conducted several experiments to compare the performance between on-site edge servers only and CollabOffloading with external clouds. The scenario of compute-intensive simulation is a calculation optimal tollgate information for vehicles driving through congested traffic situation. The results of experiments show that CollabOffloading method decreases the execution time of simulations. Furthermore, we developed web-based graphical user interface module to visualize whole process of the proposed algorithm. It is helpful to monitor resource status of Kubernetes cluster in real-time. For further work, the analysis of utilization of on-site edge servers with cloud servers is considered.

Acknowledgement. This work was supported by Institute of Information & communications Technology Planning & Evaluation(IITP) grant funded by the Korea government(MSIT) (No. 2020-0-00844, Development of Lightweight System Software Technology for Resource Management and Control of Edge Server Systems).

References

1. Nam, S.: The impact of 5G multi-access edge computing cooperation announcement on the telecom operators' firm value. 44(4), 588–598 ETRI J. (2022)
2. Yu, B., Hu, W., Xu, L., Tang, J., Liu, S., Zhu, Y.: Building the computing system for autonomous micromobility vehicles: design constraints and architectural optimizations. In: 53rd IEEE/ACM International Symposium on Microarchitecture, pp. 1067–1081. Global Online Event (2020)
3. Lee, J., Kang, S., Jeon, J., Chun, I.: Multiaccess edge computing-based simulation as a service for 5G mobile applications: a case study of tollgate selection for autonomous vehicles. Wirel. Commun. Mob. Comput (2020)
4. Rosendo, D., Silve, P., Simonin, M., Çostan, A., Antoniu, G.: E2Clab: exploring the computing continuum through repeatable, replicable and reproducible edge-to-cloud experiments. In: 2020 IEEE International Conference on Cluster Computing, Kobe, Japan, pp. 176–186 (2020)
5. Balouek-Thomert, D., Renart, E.G., Zamani, A.R., Simonet, A., Parashar, M.: Towards a computing continuum: enabling edge-to-cloud integration for data-driven workflows. Int. J. High Perform. Comput. Appl. 33(6), 1159–1174 (2019)
6. Ella, P., Arun, S., Tero, P.: Towards real-time learning for edge-cloud continuum with vehicular computing. In: IEEE 7th World Forum on Internet of Things, New Orleans, LA, United States, pp. 921–926 (2021)
7. Kubernetes. https://kubernetes.io/. Accessed 08 July 2022
8. Kubernetes Scheduling Framework. https://kubernetes.io/docs/concepts/scheduling-eviction/scheduling-framework/. Accessed 08 July 2022
9. Kubernetes Scheduler Plugins. https://kubernetes.io/docs/reference/scheduling/config. Accessed 08 July 2022
10. Amazon Web Services. https://aws.amazon.com/. Accessed 08 July 2022
11. Google Cloud Platform. https://cloud.google.com/. Accessed 08 July 2022
12. Microsoft Azure. https://azure.microsoft.com. Accessed 08 July 2022
13. Naver Cloud. https://www.navercloudcorp.com/. Accessed 08 July 2022
14. Calico. https://projectcalico.docs.tigera.io/about/about-calico. Accessed 08 July 2022

15. Mahadevan, S.: Monte Carlo simulation. Mechanical Engineering-New York and Basel-Marcel Dekker, pp. 123–146 (1997)
16. kube-ops-view. https://github.com/hjacobs/kube-ops-view. Accessed 08 July 2022

Experiments on the Battle Trend and Result of Combat21 Model and VBS4

Jonggill Lee[✉], Heenam Lee, Koangsu Lee, Hongpil Choi, Seungmin Lee, and Jaeho Im

Korea Army Training and Doctrine Command (TRADOC), Daejeon, Republic of Korea
rokleejg@gmail.com

Abstract. Recently, the Republic of Korea Army Training and Doctrine Command (TRADOC) deployed a virtual war game platform Virtual Battlespace 4(VBS4) to complement limitations of current wargame simulators. The ROK Army is utilizing VBS4 to promote competency of various virtual training in education and training fields. Accordingly, Characterizing and comparing the core behavior model between VBS4 and the traditional wargame model are highly demanded for measuring their effectiveness. This research presents the assessment of two representative military simulation software, Combat21 model and VBS4, by observing their various aspects, including procedures and results of close combat simulation. In accordance with the convergence of opinions from KCTC observers, we were able to confirm that the VBS4 replicates the real battlespace realistically compared to the Combat21 model based on comparison of each trait of the model.

Keywords: VBS4 · Combat21 model · Wargame · Modeling and simulation

1 Introduction

1.1 Research Background

As new technologies have been advanced, and pervasive due to the fourth wave, people have adopted applications of new technologies as a big part of their lives, so did the army. The army has endeavored to modernize its science and technology systems to follow the trend of the fourth wave. Especially, the deployment of science and technology in the army's training fields, has been demanded for efficiency and effectiveness of the modern battle drill constrained by reduced forces, warfight resources, and live training environments. Recently, the Republic of Korea Army TRADOC adopted a new virtual platform, VBS4, to demonstrate the effectiveness of the virtual training and performed some research to find out specific training areas that can be applied to this new platform.

1.2 Motivation

As mentioned in Sect. 1.1, the Republic of Korea Army TRADOC has endeavored to adequately apply and measure VBS4 in various training fields after its deployment.

© Springer Nature Singapore Pte Ltd. 2022
B.-Y. Chang and C. Choi (Eds.): AsiaSim 2021, CCIS 1636, pp. 56–67, 2022.
https://doi.org/10.1007/978-981-19-6857-0_6

Especially, the need for leveraging training capability in the constructive domain has been demanded rather than the virtual aspects, since it can be utilized on various fields in tactical perspective that can effectively measure competency of the trainee for a whole training period.

Since constructive domain training provides various virtual battlespace to participants of the simulator with its simulated battlespace by interconnecting various operation features from individual to brigade levels. There is no doubt that thorough analysis of simulated models of a single entity is taking the one of crucial roles for simulator assessment. This research was motivated to measure training capabilities and its effectiveness of VBS4 compared to an obsolescence simulator model, Combat 21 model, that have been used in the ROK Army for a couple decades. Especially, the research was focused on the elapsed time, trends, and results of the force-on-force close combats that sufficiently reflects the feature of each simulator. These aspects represent core functionalities of constructive models since realistic replication of the fair fight is the primary virtue for warfight trainees. The VBS4 provides free maneuvering features to entities with a vast combat environment that has fundamental differences compared to obsolete constructive training models. The Combat21 model, on the other hand, periodically assesses damage in the unit level with Lanchester's loss factor based mathematical model. Therefore, realizing the core difference between each simulator, and making a fair comparison for specific training cases are required steps for leveraging the training effectiveness of the proposed simulator deployment.

1.3 Method

As mentioned in the previous section, multiple combat experiments were conducted by using the Combat21 model and VBS4. Various aspects of data of the force-on-force close combat have been measured in real time. The assessment was conducted by comparing procedures and results with repeated force-on-force close combats with the same scale of units on each faction in the same battlespace. There were prior studies that measured effectiveness of the Combat21 model. Based on [3], a study extended the training methodology by linking K1 tank simulator to the Combat21 model [3]. Recently, imposing adequate damage impact to the model by applying machine learning has been proposed [4], however, no direct comparison between VBS4 and Combat21 has been made (comparing newly deployed model to obsolete model).

1.4 Scope

The experiment was conducted for direct comparison between VBS4, and Combat21 model with various aspects of combat elements, and the range of the experiment was defined concisely, as shown in Table 1, which has combat elements such as elapsed time, trend, and results of the force-on-force close combats. The boundary of the range was defined by discussing with four experienced initiatives managers, and experts in terms of simulator features that make differences on the simulation result.

Table 1. Scope and details of the combat experiment.

Experimental region	Focus	Criterion
Battle time	Battle start and end times	Start and end of the fire
Battle trend	Damage status during battle time	Update every 5 min
Battle result	Battle result, victory or defeat	Judgment criteria

2 Introduction of the Wargame Models

2.1 Combat21 model

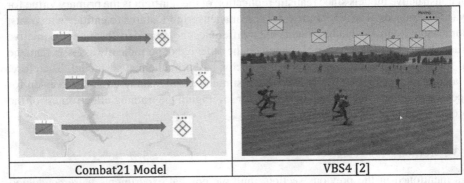

| Combat21 Model | VBS4 [2] |

Fig. 1. Wargame models. Conceptual figure of Combat21 model (left). Conceptual figure of VBS4 (right).

Combat21 model has been developed to provide simulation feature of small unit combats for the battle command and control at brigade or battalion levels to Commanders and Staffs, and it supports various modeling features such as command/control and communication, information, maneuver, fire, combat supports, etc. [1]. The model simulates combat operation function reflecting combat support equipment, and combat related unit characteristic values of each units, with mathematical modeling as a pillar.

Most of the battle damage assessment (BDA) in constructive models are hardly operable in real time with short amount of sampling intervals, therefore, provide mathematically computed results with large time intervals (e.g. 5 min). Equation 1 represents an example of BDA in constructive model:

$$\Delta X_{ij} = a_{ij} \times Y_{avail(i)}$$

$$Y_{avail(i)} = F_{sr} \times V \times F_{nc(j)} \times Y_i \tag{1}$$

ΔX_{ij}: Damage of army unit j by army unit i
a_{ij}: Lanchester's loss factor from i to j
$Y_{avail(i)}$: The number of operable agents in army unit i

F_{sr}: Combat power quota(%) - level of combat power assignment to assault direction
V: Vulnerability element coefficient - vulnerability of army unit accounting to its status
$F_{nc(j)}$: Damage damping coefficient according to its encampment
Y_i: The number of agents in army unit i

BDA computing formula can be customized by traits of force, weapon systems, and Indirect fires (artillery), however, BDA of Combat 21 follows the direct fire based, traditional close force-on-force combat formula shown in Eq. 1. As traditional constructive models, the model provides BDA once in a given time interval.

2.2 VBS4

VBS4 provides various types of virtual training environments by customizing scenarios in a huge geological domain, called VBS World Server (VWS). Every mission from VBS4 can be produced and conducted by proceeding with training preparation, execution, and assessment stages that resemble the steps in army's training. Players of the VBS4 can easily plan out, generate, and redact battlespace and experience combat with given environments [2].

2.2.1 Behavior Tree (BT) Based Computer Generated Force (CGF) Modelling in VBS4

Modeling behavior of warfighting soldiers in the real battlefield is very challenging, and hard to grasp its decision-making process, and creativity since the experience in the real battlefield can be unique. In the early stage of CGF generation, the most widely used behavior model was based on Finite State Machines (FSMs) that were well suitable for pre-define rule based constructive entities in military simulation systems. The FSMs, however, have been hard to manage due to its exponentially increased complexity of states with the increment of non-mutually exclusive behaviors from a number of entities [4].

Accounting for the issue of FSMs, Behavior Trees have been proposed, and become one of a powerful, and popular technique for developing behavior models for automated constructive entities in military simulation systems. BTs have similar traits that FSMs have, however, their main building blocks are tasks based rather than states that significantly reduce the overall complexity of CGFs behavior modeling. This makes BTs highly modular, easily composable, and human readable. These benefits of BTs provide utilization capability for automatic generation using machine learning techniques [5, 6].

VBS4 accepts BTs for constructing its behavior models of CGF using VBS control. As can be seen, Fig. 2 is presenting a simple example of BT in VBS control. BTs are graphically represented as directed rooted trees that are composed of nodes and edges that connect the nodes. For a pair of connected nodes, the outgoing node is called the parent, and the incoming node is called the child. A parent node can contain one or more children. Rooted trees have one parentless node that is called the root. Nodes without children are called leaves. A BT represents all the possible courses of action an agent can take. The BT defines possible action of an unmounted maneuvering soldier [7].

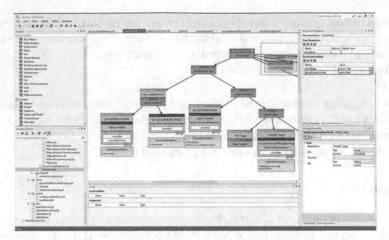

Fig. 2. Behavior Tree based CGF control editor [2].

3 Experiments

3.1 Experimental Plan and Environment Setting

The experiment was conducted by setting up force-on-force close combat scenarios with units expecting imminent contact with the adversaries of each unit. Environmental settings such as Table 2 removed extra elements that aren't directly related to the combat, and do not clearly reflect the methodology of the model behavior.

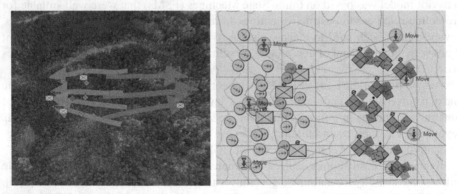

Fig. 3. VBS4 experiment setup in 3D view (left), and 2D map (right). Each faction group (BLUFOR,OPFOR) engaged each other in a sudden during maneuver.

Table 2. Experimental settings

Division	Settings
Day and night	Day
Weather	Sunny
Terrain	Forest
Location	Random Area(South Korea)
Unit size	Platoon
Unit equipment	Rifles, machine guns and firearms
Experimental method	Attack(BLUFOR) and defense(OPFOR)
Number of experiments	30(forward10, side 10, rear 10)
Scenario	A battle between the moving BLUFOR and the defending OPFOR in anticipation of the presence of the enemy
Battle time	Time from the first shot to the last shot
Victory and defeat	1. If one unit is destroyed, the unit that is not destroyed wins. 2. If there is a large margin of casualties and the battle is over

For example, practically the adversaries which took over the base used to behave defensively. However, this might affect the force-on-force contact results. Therefore, no special defensive stance has been applied in this experiment. The force-on-force close combats were done from front, lateral, and rear side for 10 times each. Location of the units, stance, weather, and terrain were confined to be the same for whole experiments. For fair comparison, both simulators generated identical composition of CGFs of BLUFOR, and OPFOR.

3.2 Measured Results

3.2.1 The Results of the Battle Time Comparison

The basic statistical amount of the close combat experiment result is shown in Table 3 based on the elapsed combat time set in the environmental setting, in Sect. 2.2.

As can be seen, the least elapsed combat time of the VBS4 ranged from 2 min to 11 min, whereas the elapsed combat time of the Combat21 model took more than 50 min. In other words, the elapsed time spent on the VBS4 was much less than that of the Combat21 model. The observation trend of the elapsed combat time for each simulator model is shown in Fig. 4 that depicts a histogram of the elapsed combat time for each model. The difference of the closed combat time was attributed by the characteristics difference of each simulator model. The blue bar on the left is the result of VBS4 and the orange bar on the right is the Combat21 model.

Table 3. Elapsed combat time

	Group	minimum time	maximum time	mode	mean	VAR	STD
VBS4	A(forward)	2	10	3	4.70	8.46	2.91
	B(side)	3	11	4	5.30	5.79	2.41
	C(rear)	3	11	3	6.50	8.72	2.95
	Integrated	2	11	3	5.50	8.72	2.78
Combat 21 model	A(forward)	35	55	45	44.50	30.28	5.50
	B(side)	35	64	50	52.50	72.94	8.54
	C(rear)	41	65	55	53.00	48.00	6.93
	Integrated	35	65	45	50.00	62.62	7.91

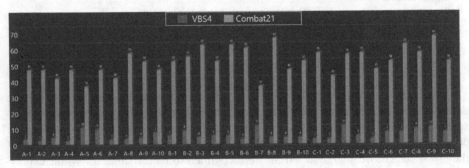

Fig. 4. Combat time test result(min)

Combat21 model calculates damage by using a mathematical model, Lanchester's loss factor once per each cycle (5–10 min) that leverages the amount of damage based on the number of units, type of weapon and ammo, and their effectiveness for each faction. The VBS4 model, on the other hand, applies damage in real time generated from the close combat. The interview was conducted with experts, 9 KCTC platoon level observers, to confirm how much the close combat result from each simulator well reflects the real battlespace training environment.

Based on experiences of KCTC live combat training of each expert, the elapsed combat time was uniformly spaded ranged from <20 min to 60 min, however, those replies were assuming that various effects applied on the close combat, for instance, protection and trench effect. Also, the elapsed combat time accounted for the entire elimination of the one side. Therefore, for fair determination, and interpretation, the detailed analysis about the trend of close combats has to be accompanied concurrently with the elapsed combat time.

3.2.2 Combat Trend Comparison Results

Analyzing concurrent metric of the elapsed time, and trend of the close combat helps comparing which model presents a more realistic battlespace. The trend of the close combat of VBS4 is depicted in Fig. 5. The left side of the figure shows the damage of the BLUFOR, while the left side shows the damage of the OPFOR.

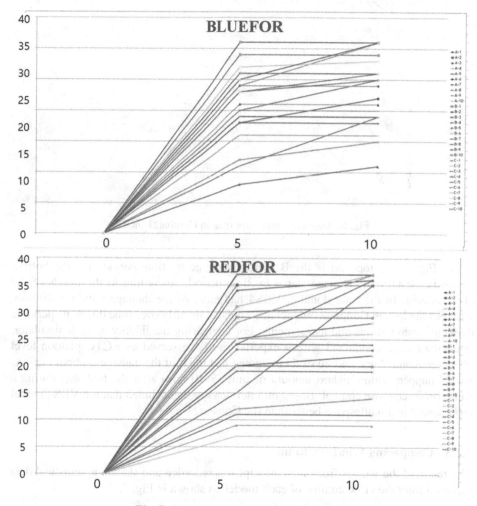

Fig. 5. Damage status over time in VBS4

Most of the damage for both factions occurred within 5 min, according to the figure. Some trials spent more time on the close combat that had relatively less damage within 5–10 mis compared to most of the trials. Also, the trend of the close combat of Combat21 model at the domain of the elapsed combat time is depicted in Fig. 6.

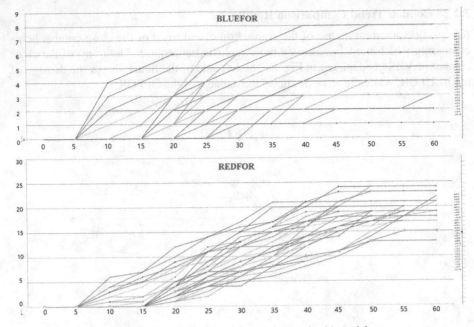

Fig. 6. Damage status over time in Combat21 model

In Fig. 3, the top part is the BLUFOR damage by time period, and the bottom figure is the OPFOR damage status by time period. According to the trends of the close combat in the time domain, VBS4 had most of the damage within 5–10 min, whereas the loss in Combat21 model accumulated linearly over time due to its periodic damage computations and assessments. For comparing the fidelity of each simulator, interviews were conducted with 9 experts who have served as KCTC platoon level observers/controllers, and all of them agreed that most of the damage on both factions would happen within a short amount of time (5–10 min) after the first shot during a force-on-force close combat. Based on interviews, we concluded that the VBS4 model represented real battlespace better than the Combat21 model.

3.2.3 Comparing Win/Loss Ratio

The result of the winner from each attempt was recorded and shown as statistical data received from the close combat of each model, as shown in Fig. 7.

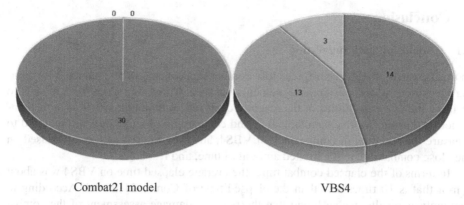

Combat21 model   VBS4

Fig. 7. Win and loss results according to the model

In Fig. 7, blue shows the victory of BLUFOR, orange shows the win of OPFOR, and finally, gray shows the case of a draw. As can be seen, BLUEFOR and OPFOR won 14, and 13 combats out of 30, respectively, and had 3 ties. In the Combat21 model, however, BLUFOR won all combat. We presumed that these results were based on the characteristics of each model. The VBS4 has a behavior tree based free maneuvering that can cause various results on the close combats, however, Lanchester's loss factor mathematical computation based model, Combat 21 model, provides identical value that unlikely give difference on the battle result when the scale of the unit, and weapon is the same.

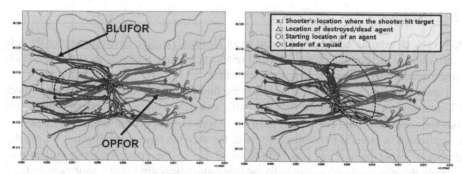

Fig. 8. 2D map images of close combat experiments. The setup of the experiment is identical. An experiment when OPFOR won the close combat (left). An experiment when OPFOR won the close combat (right).

Post simulation result of force-on-force close combat experiment is shown in 2D map image, as shown in Fig. 8. As can be seen, even with identical experiment setup, each trial gave different combat results in terms of trend of won/loss, and number of casualties. Each sub-figure in Fig. 8 shows trace of remained agents after the fierce combat (dashed circle in the figure) that implies result of the close combat.

4 Conclusion

4.1 Conclusion and Suggestion

In this research, the force-on-force close combat experiments were conducted for comparing various aspects of combat elements between VBS4, and Combat21 models to analyze training capabilities of the recently deployed war simulator, VBS4 in the constructive domain. More characterization and comparison of simulators are required to measure the potential of competency of VBS4, however, the research only focused on the close combat due to the limited amount of time, and resources.

In terms of the elapsed combat time, the average elapsed time on VBS4 was about 5 min that is 10 times less than the elapsed time of Combat21 model. According to the analysis results, we've found that the periodic damage assessment of the combat model contributed to the elapsed time differences between Combat21 model, and VBS4. Furthermore, in terms of the combat trend, most of the battle damage occurred within 5 min of the initial engagement in VBS4, whereas the damage increased linearly every 5 to 10 min period in the Combat21 model. That difference is attributed by the model characteristics of each simulator model.

When it comes to the combat results, BLUFOR units won every force-on-force close combat in Combat21 model, whereas both factions (BLUFOR, and OPFOR) won battles for 14 and 13 times respectively and had 3 ties in VBS4.

Variance of combat results in VBS4 presents that the procedures and results of the close combats were affected by various variables in the battlespace, such as the magnificent degree of freedom of the maneuver control of a single entity.

4.2 Limitations

This research conducted the experiment in an identical, simple environment for the fair comparison of the combat procedures and results between Combat21 model, and VBS4. Some limitations existed due to some constraints.

First of all, the scale, and scenarios were limited. The platoon-level close contact of Gathering force happens on the real battle space, therefore, generalizing the result from the scenario to the real battlespace has a limitation. Second, scenarios might not be applicable in general battlespace because the weapon types were limited. Third, the number of experiment trials was limited to 30 due to the operation environment that supports the war game simulators. To establish statistical credibility, more attempts of experiment are potentially required.

In future works, those limitations would be resolved by closing the gap between the virtual battlespace environment and the real battlespace with the enhanced number of experiment trials. Despite the limitations we faced, this research was valuable because we analyzed and compared various aspects of each model through close combat experiments which have never been conducted so far.

References

1. Joint Chiefs of Staff: War Game List book, pp. 43–48 (2015)
2. www.bisimulations.com (2016)
3. Ko, S.-G., Lee, T.-E., Kim, D.-K., Choi, M.-S.: Interoperability between Combat 21 and K1 tank simulators using a converter. J. Korea Inst. Military Sci. Technol. **13**(5), 841–851 (2010)
4. Mo, H.: A study on an expert system for close combat battlefield situation assessment in war-game models using machine learning. Korean J. Military Art Sci. **74**(3), 315–335 (2018)
5. Evensen, P.-I., et al.: Modeling battle drills for computer-generated forces using behavior trees. In: Proceedings of the Interservice/Industry Training, Simulation and Education Conference (I/ITSEC) (2018)
6. Dompke, U.: Computer Generated Forces – Background, Defenition and Basic Technologies. RTO-SAS Lecture series on "Simulation of and for Military Decision Making (2001)
7. Abbott, R.G.: Trainable automated forces. In: Proceedings of the Interservice/Industry Training", Simulation and Education Conference (I/ITSEC) (2010)

A Study on SES-Based Information Security Framework for Autonomous Vehicle Controlling Environment

Hyung-Jong Kim[✉] ⓘ and Hwahyeon Park ⓘ

Seoul Women's University, Seoul 01779, South Korea
{hkim,0425pipi}@swu.ac.kr

Abstract. Currently information security matters in controlling the autonomous vehicles in terms of communication among autonomous vehicles and controller systems. In this work, we are proposing a secure communication framework which is operating on SES (System Entity Structure) concept. In Particular, we represented all the attributes of the autonomous vehicles and a controller using the SES concept. In addition, we presented how the encryption and decryption can be proceeded using attributes which are gathered from the SES instance. The contribution of this work is showing a way of making use of SES for securing the communication among participating entities.

Keywords: System entity structure · Autonomous vehicle · Security framework

1 Introduction

SEA (Society of Automotive Engineers) announced the evaluation criteria for autonomous vehicle's technological maturity [1]. According to the criteria, in higher levels of maturity, drivers of vehicles are less involved in controlling vehicles and the car driving process has high dependence on various sensors and controllers of autonomous vehicles. In addition, the control center for autonomous vehicles has an important role of providing autonomous vehicles with data related to road traffic, accidents on the road and so on. For this reason, the communication traffic volume for operating autonomous vehicles is way too large and as the level of maturity is getting higher, the amount of communication traffic volume is getting larger. According to [2], the communication traffic volume is estimated as 3 GB per a second and 1.4 TB per an hour at low level maturity. On the other hand, at the high level maturity, it is estimated as 40 GB per a second and 19 TB per an hour. Because of this large volume of data transferring, it is inevitable to face the risk related to the data secrecy and integrity. According to the vulnerability which is identified with CVE-2021-3347, a drone could open the car door by accessing the Wi-Fi [3]. When we look into the incidents on autonomous vehicles since 2010, we could see that the incidents related to servers for the autonomous vehicles take 32.94% and the attack from remote places dominantly takes 79.6% compared to physical access which takes 20.7% [4]. Based on these statistics, we recognized that the

© Springer Nature Singapore Pte Ltd. 2022
B.-Y. Chang and C. Choi (Eds.): AsiaSim 2021, CCIS 1636, pp. 68–73, 2022.
https://doi.org/10.1007/978-981-19-6857-0_7

secure communication among autonomous vehicles and controller servers is essential for secure and safe operation of autonomous vehicles.

In this work, we propose an SES (System Entity Structure) based security framework which exploits pairing-based encryption schemes. The SES based security framework enables users to embed the complex structure of the autonomous vehicle environment for the encryption and decryption procedures. When encryption is conducted, the structural knowledge is embedded into the ciphertext. On the other hand, when decryption is conducted the receiver's structural information is compared with the structural information in the ciphertext. Based on this encryption and decryption scheme, we present how the scheme can be applied for secure communication of autonomous vehicle environments.

2 Related Works

The autonomous vehicle environment is operating on the basis of various sensors' fusion. The sensors are reflecting the current situation with quantified values and some of the values should be kept as secret for their purposes. In [5], the CP-ABE algorithm is deployed for encrypting context attributes which consists of various values measured by various sensors. By applying the CP-ABE for encryption of the sensor fusion environment, [5] shows how the dynamically changing structured values can be encrypted and decrypted. [6] presents an IoT environment which is working on a blockchain framework. Since blockchain is only focusing on the integrity of the data, [6] shows that application of attribute-based encryption can enhance the security of the IoT environment.

The SES concept has been used for describing the structural knowledge of a system and enables engineers to configure the structure of the system dynamically before it starts working. [7] made use of the SES concept for configuring the performance evaluation scenarios of blockchain based services. The experiment compares two different configurations of a service and the SES concept is applied well for accomplishing the purpose. The SES concept is well applied to wireless sensor networks which is similar to the autonomous vehicle environment. In [8], for the flexible design and convenient experiment of large scale sensor networks, the SES and the PES which is a pruned version of SES are presented. In addition, [8] shows the SES and PES concept can help users to manage computer models more effectively by storing them into the model base. To develop a simulation model for experiment, the developer needs to focus on the definition of unit model and the composition of unit models. In addition, the developer needs to have a novel way to represent the experiment scenarios which are supposed to be applied to the simulation model. [9] shows how the component unit models can be defined and connected to represent the cyberattack and defense scenarios. The presentation of the attack and defense of [9] is referable in this work for composing the autonomous vehicles service scenarios.

3 Autonomous Vehicle Controlling Environment

3.1 Service Scenarios of Autonomous Vehicles

At SAE's maturity level 5 of autonomous vehicles, the entire system should be able to control vehicles and take into account the traffic status of roads. Figure 1 shows the scenario of the control system at the SAE level 5 maturity. The autonomous vehicle environment consists of three objects such as users, vehicles, and the monitoring center. In this scenario, users make use of a vehicle sharing service and the autonomous vehicles are controlled by the monitoring center. As users request the vehicle sharing service, they send the origin, destination and number of passengers to the monitoring center. Upon the request from users, the monitoring center dispatches a proper vehicle to the location where the users are. In this situation, the monitoring center needs to be able to look into the users personal data and vehicles secret data. In the user's data case, there can be a personal identification number or payment related information. In the vehicle data case, there can be photos and sensor data from devices which are installed in autonomous vehicles. Even if the monitoring center can read those kinds of data, while they are transferring through a communication channel, the confidentiality of the data should be preserved.

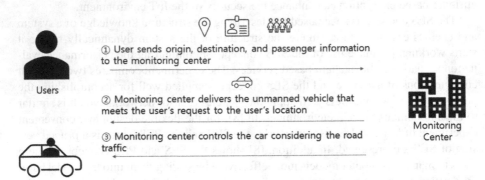

Fig. 1. Services scenario of autonomous vehicles

3.2 SES Structure

Figure 2 shows the SES representation of the Autonomous Vehicle Sharing Service. The service entity is decomposed into users, vehicles and monitoring center entities. In addition, the vehicle entity has type, components and sensors entities. The type is the terminal entity and has the value for representing the vehicle type such as sedan, coupe and so on. The components entity has terminal entities such as fuel, engine, wheel and seat. These four entities contain their own values for representation of a car entity. Lastly, the sensors entity has three different sensors such as GPS, Lidar and camera entities for containing the measured environment information. The monitoring center has the location entity which is decomposed into route number, longitude and latitude for representation of vehicle's location. In addition, the traffic entity contains the traffic volume for choosing an economic route from origin to destination. The User entity has the origin and destination entities for deciding the route and the passenger information for charging the fee.

The vehicle would transfer the sensor data to the monitoring center and the users would transfer their service request to the monitoring center with their personal information. In these data transferring cases, some of the data should be protected for preserving the security and privacy of the cars on the road and the passengers of the autonomous vehicles.

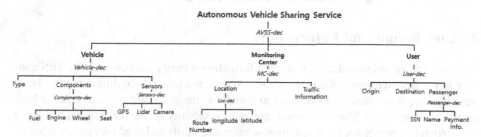

Fig. 2. SES structure of autonomous vehicle sharing service

In this protection scenario, we can use the SES structure for encrypting the data and instances of vehicle, monitoring center and user are supposed to be used for decrypting the data. Figure 3 shows three different parts which are used for decrypting the data in our SES-based information security framework.

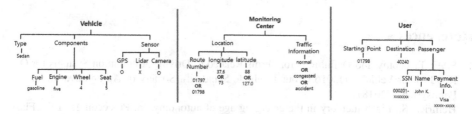

Fig. 3. Instance of entity from SES for decryption

Figure 4 shows the matching between SES and the instance for data decryption. If the instance matches with SES and the decryption key is proper, the decryption succeeds. Only with the proper decryption key, the decryption cannot succeed.

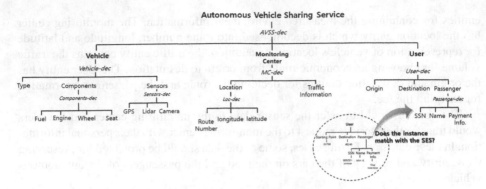

Fig. 4. Matching between a instance with SES structure

4   Conclusions and Future Work

In this work, we proposed a SES-based information security framework. The SES concept is for representation of a system's structural knowledge. In addition, the attribute-based encryption scheme can be used to match the instance information with the SES structure information. The SES-based information security framework is designed using this structural knowledge representation scheme and attribute-based encryption scheme.

Currently we are developing the SES-based encryption scheme to apply the suggested concept for an autonomous vehicle sharing service. While we are developing the scheme, we would evaluate the performance of the scheme and compare it with other existing encryption and decryption schemes.

Acknowledgements. This research was partially supported by Basic Science Research Program through the National Research Foundation of Korea (NRF) funded by the Ministry of Science and ICT (NRF-2021R1F1A1055522).

References

1. SAE: Taxonomy and Definitions for Terms Related to Driving Automation Systems for On-Road Motor Vehicles (J3016 Ground Vehicle Standard). Society of Automotive Engineers, Pennsylvania (2018)
2. Heinrich, S.: Flash memory in the emerging age of autonomy. In: Proceedings of the Flash Memory Summit, Flash Memory Summit 2017, pp. 7–10. Santa Clara, USA (2017)
3. Weinmann, R., Schmotzle, B.: TBONE – A zero-click exploit for Tesla MCUs, v1.0, Comsecuris (2020)
4. Global Automotive Cybersecurity Report 2021: Upstream Security (2021)
5. Song, Y., Seo, A., Lee, J., Kim, Y.: Access control policy of data considering varying context in sensor fusion environment of Internet of Things. KIPS Trans. Software Data Eng. **4**(9), 409–418 (2015)
6. Rahulamathavan, Y., Phan, R., Rajarajan, M., Misra, S., Kondoz, A.: Privacy-preserving blockchain based IoT ecosystem using attribute-based encryption. In: 2017 IEEE International Conference on Advanced Networks and Telecommunications Systems (ANTS), pp. 1–6 (2017)

7. Kim, T., Kim, H.-J.: DEVS-based Experimental Framework for Blockchain Services. Simulation Modelling Practice and Theory, vol. 108, no 1 (2021)
8. Nam, S.M., Kim, H.J.: WSN-SES/MB: system entity structure and model base framework for large-scale wireless sensor networks. Sensors **21**, 430 (2021)
9. Kim, J., Kim, H.: DEVS-based modeling methodology for cybersecurity simulations from a security perspective. KSII Trans. Internet Inf. Syst. **14**(5), 2186–2203 (2020). https://doi.org/10.3837/tiis.2020.05.018

Cross-Retransmission Techniques in Licensed and Unlicensed Spectrum Bands over Wireless Access Networks

Eunkyung Kim[✉][iD]

Department of Artificial Intelligence Software, Hanbat National University,
125, Dongseo-daero, Yuseong-gu, Daejeon 34158, Korea
ekim@hanbat.ac.kr

Abstract. In this paper, we propose HARQ retransmission algorithms in the wireless access networks exploiting not only licensed spectrum band but also unlicensed spectrum band with meeting the regulatory requirements such as Listen-Before-Talk. In particular, the proposed HARQ retransmission via one available component carrier regardless of the spectrum is licensed or unlicensed is beneficial in a sense that it doesn't increase the transmission latency with potential retransmissions. We also show that the proposed algorithm achieves lower transmission latency without increasing HARQ RTT through the simulation.

Keywords: Wireless networks · Latency reduction · HARQ retransmission · Unlicensed spectrum channel access

1 Introduction

Recently, wireless access networks are deploying to support drastically increasing network traffic. It is mainly due to the large demand on the mobile-related services including Internet of Things (IoT) service, Machine-to-Machine (M2M) service, etc. [8]. It is also shifting toward a new paradigm that enhances user's high quality of experience to provide continuous services with a large amount of data packets as well as low latency with high reliable data transmission between the application server and end-user in wireless access networks [9].

In order to provide the extremely large amount of network traffic in cellular system by improving spectral efficiency and data rates for broadband data services, 3GPP LTE [1] and NR [5] employ various enhanced techniques such as multiple antenna transmissions, carrier aggregation, interference management [11]. However, it is still difficult to catch up with the network explosion with the network capacity achieved by those techniques. In other words, the explosive increase in demand for mobile services is surpassing the improvement of spectral efficiency. Thus, more frequency bands and the wireless access techniques operated in those new frequency bands such as 5 GHz unlicensed band and mmWave band became a promising solution [10,11]. In particular, extending

© Springer Nature Singapore Pte Ltd. 2022
B.-Y. Chang and C. Choi (Eds.): AsiaSim 2021, CCIS 1636, pp. 74–85, 2022.
https://doi.org/10.1007/978-981-19-6857-0_8

LTE to 5 GHz unlicensed spectrum, which is called Licensed-Assisted Access (LAA), has attracted great attention as a means to accommodate the rapid mobile data growth. In contrast to wireless access operated typically in licensed band, LAA can be operated with a shared spectrum band, i.e., 5 GHz unlicensed band [6,10]. However, it is very complicated to operate cellular systems in unlicensed spectrum. It is due to the fact that in the wireless access network such as LTE and NR, a base station (BS), e.g., eNB, and gNB, and a mobile station (MS), e.g., UE. can enjoy the spectrum band, particularly in licensed band, without any accessing the channel for the data transmission, but those transmitters shall access the channel for the data transmission with meeting the regulatory requirements for shared spectrum band. In particular, a transmitter, e.g., eNB, gNB, and UE, shall access the channel prior to the data transmission for shared spectrum band according to either the dynamic channel access mode on the top of Load Based Equipment (LBE) or the semi-static channel access mode on the top of Frame Based Equipment (FBE) [3,7]. In both channel access modes for the shared spectrum, the transmitter may apply Listen-Before-Talk (LBT) prior to performing a transmission on a cell configured with the shared spectrum channel access. In addition, it is considered that access to the shared spectrum shall be in compliance with regulatory requirements, including: (i) Clear Channel Assessment (CCA) as part of LBT operation shall be performed to ensure that the channel is not in use by any other device including initial data transmission as well as HARQ retransmissions. If the channel is considered as available, the transmitter can transmit data on the unlicensed band and (ii) Channel Occupancy Time (COT) is limited. For instance, maximum COT is 4 ms for Japan and 10 ms for Europe. Here, the COT is the total time for which a transmitter and its corresponding receiver(s) sharing the channel occupancy perform transmission(s) on the unlicensed channel after performing a CCA.

Meanwhile, low-latency with high reliability is one of the requirements to support emerging new use cases in wireless access networks such as factory automation, intelligent transport systems, and remote medical surgery [12]. In contrast to the wireless access in the licensed spectrum where a base station and a mobile station can enjoy the spectrum band without any accessing the channel for the data transmission, LAA leads to the overhead due to the CCA for the initial transmission as an additional CCA for the contiguous transmissions when the COT expires.

Figure 1 shows an example of transmission and retransmission in an unlicensed component carrier (UCC), where maximum COT and feedbacks corresponding to the downlink transmissions are assumed to be no more than 10 subframe lengths and to be transmitted via licensed component carrier (LCC), respectively. As shown in the example, HARQ retransmission for the last part of the COT may not be performed within the COT, which means additional CCA needs to occupy the channel for the HARQ retransmission. It is due to the fact that data transmission (possibly including HARQ retransmission) in unlicensed bands shall be performed with meeting the regulatory requirement, which is the CCA shall be performed whenever the occupied channel access time exceeds

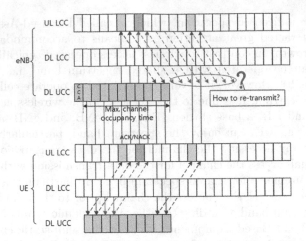

Fig. 1. An example of HARQ retransmission in shared spectrum, where LCC and UCC denote licensed component carrier and unlicensed component carrier, respectively. Maximum COT is assumed to be no more than 10 subframe lengths (i.e., 10 ms) and response for the downlink data transmission is assumed to be fed back via LCC.

the maximum allowed COT. Hence, inspired by the question *how to offer HARQ retransmission service in unlicensed spectrum*, we propose HARQ retransmission process in unlicensed spectrum as follows: (i) retransmission is only performed via UCC, (ii) retransmission is only performed via LCC, and (iii) retransmission is performed via one of any available CC (including LCC and UCC). In particular, the proposed cross-carrier retransmissions allowing the transmitter to perform retransmissions via either LCC or one of any available component carriers (CCs) including LCC and UCC can provide low-latency retransmission.

The rest of this paper is organised as follows: In the following section, we describe the channel access mechanism in unlicensed spectrum. In Sect. 3, we propose HARQ retransmission algorithms in unlicensed spectrum. Next, we compare the performance of the proposed algorithms via simulation in Sect. 4. Finally, we conclude this paper in Sect. 5.

2   Channel Access Mechanism in Unlicensed Spectrum

In this section, we summarise the channel access mechanism, adaptivity described in [3]. Here, adaptivity means that an automatic channel access mechanism by which a device avoids transmissions in a channel in the presence of transmissions from other devices in that channel. In other words, adaptivity is intended to be used to detect transmissions from other devices operating in the unlicensed bands.

In unlicensed spectrum bands according to the regulatory requirements, a device shall access the channel prior to the data transmission for shared spectrum band according to one of the channel access modes. Figure 2 shows the channel

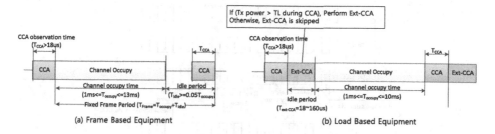

Fig. 2. Channel access modes in unlicensed spectrum band. (a) Frame Based Equipment (FBE). (b) Load Based Equipment (LBE).

access mode, which is performed semi-statically on the top of Frame Based Equipment (FBE) or dynamically on the top of Load Based Equipment (LBE).

For the semi-statical channel access mode based on FBE (see Fig. 2(a)), a device, which is intending to start transmissions on an operating channel in an unlicensed spectrum band, shall perform a clear channel assessment (CCA) check using energy detection for a duration of the time, i.e., CCA observation time (e.g., 18 μs). During the given time, if the energy level in the channel exceeds the threshold corresponding to the power level given as a CCA threshold level, the operating channel is considered occupied by another device. In this case, the device considers the channel is occupied and shall not transmit on that channel during the next Fixed Frame Period. Otherwise (i.e., if the device finds the operating channel to be clear), it is allowed to transmit data immediately. In addition, for a device having simultaneous transmissions on that channel, the device is allowed to continue transmissions on the given the channel without re-evaluating the availability of that channel. Here, the total allowed time is defined as Channel Occupancy Time (COT), which is given in range 1 ms to 10 ms, e.g., 4 ms for Japan and 10 ms for Europe. Towards the end of the Idle Period, the device shall perform a new CCA as described above, where the minimum Idle Period shall be at least 5% of the Channel Occupancy Time used by the device for the current Fixed Frame Period.

In contrast to FBE which is based on the semi-statical channel access, LBE (see Fig. 2(b)) is a dynamic Listen-Before-Talk (LBT) based spectrum sharing mechanism based on the CCA mode using energy detect, as described in IEEE 802.11 [4]. Similar to the channel mode based on FBE, a device performs a CCA check using energy detection whether to decided the channel is occupied or clear. Instead of trying CCA to transmit on that channel during the next Fixed Frame Period in FBE, the device performs an Extended CCA (Ext-CCA) check in which the operating channel is observed for a random duration in the range between 18 μs and at least 160 μs. During the Ext-CCA check, if there are no transmissions, the period is considered as the Idle Period in between transmissions. If the Ext-CCA check has determined the channel to be no longer occupied, the device may resume transmissions on this channel. The device is

78   E. Kim

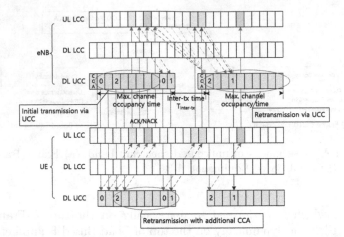

Fig. 3. An example of HARQ retransmission in shared spectrum, where retransmission is performed via UCC. Maximum COT is assumed to be no more than 10 subframe lengths (i.e., 10 ms) and response for the downlink data transmission is assumed to be fed back via LCC. Also, inter-tx time is assumed to be 4 ms due to additional CCA.

also allowed to continue transmission on the channel within the providing the COT, which is the same as that in FBE.

3 HARQ Retransmissions in Licensed and Unlicensed Spectrum

In this section, we propose HARQ retransmission process in licensed component carrier (LCC) and unlicensed component carrier (UCC) over wireless access networks where the LCC is the licensed frequency band operated as a primary component carrier and UCC is the unlicensed frequency carrier operated as a secondary component carrier. For simplicity, we assume that initial transmission is performed at the beginning of the COT after the channel is occupied after CCA. Also, the CCA is assumed to be terminated right before the subframe for the data transmission starts.

3.1 HARQ Retransmission via UCC

Figure 3 shows an example of the HARQ retransmissions via UCC, where the UCC is the same as the component carrier (CC) of initial transmission. We also assume that the maximum COT is to be 10 ms. As shown in the example, HARQ retransmission of the beginning parts of COT (e.g., HARQ Process ID #0) can be performed without additional CCA to re-occupy the same UCC. In other words, the HARQ retransmission for the HARQ Process ID #0 can be performed prior to the expiry of the COT. For instance, on the other hand, HARQ retransmission for HARQ Process ID #2 may not be performed within

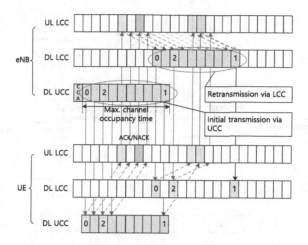

Fig. 4. An example of HARQ retransmission in shared spectrum, where retransmission is performed via LCC. Maximum COT is assumed to be no more than 10 subframe lengths (i.e., 10 ms) and response for the downlink data transmission is assumed to be fed back via LCC.

the COT. Instead, the HARQ retransmission may be delayed due to limited COT as well as additional CCA until the channel is determined as "idle." Thus, we propose the modification of HARQ process such as HARQ RTT timer[1], especially in the case of synchronous HARQ and/or long latency exceeding HARQ RTT timer due to consecutive un-accessible (i.e., busy) channel as the result of CCA. The modified HARQ RTT timer can be expressed by:

$$\min\{\max\{8, (K_i\%8) + T_{inter-tx}\}, max\_RTT\}, \tag{1}$$

where K_i and max_RTT denote the index from the last subframe within maximum channel occupancy time and preconfigured maximum RTT timer, respectively. Note that if the latency due to the CCA is greater than the max_RTT, data transmission is failed and the transmitter may re-initiate new transmission.

The main advantages of this HARQ retransmission via UCC are the same as the legacy method defined in [2]. In particular, those are including: (i) independent MAC scheduler can be exploited on each CC and (ii) buffering the data in any other CC for the UCC is not needed. On the other hand, disadvantages of this approach include (i) it may be hard to perform retransmission in the same UCC due to limited transmission duration, i.e., COT, and (ii) after maximum transmission duration, i.e., expiry of COT, additional CCA is necessary to occupy the same UCC for the retransmission via the occupying UCC.

---

[1] We assumed HARQ RTT timer is 8 subframe according to LTE [2].

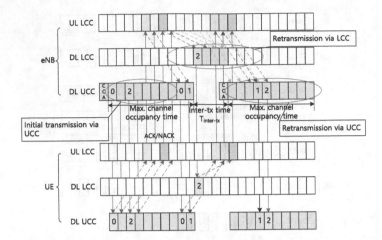

Fig. 5. An example of HARQ retransmission in shared spectrum, where retransmission is performed via any available LCC or UCC. Maximum COT is assumed to be no more than 10 subframe lengths (i.e., 10 ms) and response for the downlink data transmission is assumed to be fed back via LCC. Also, inter-tx time is assumed to be 4 ms due to additional CCA.

3.2 HARQ Retransmission via LCC

Figure 4 an example of the HARQ retransmission via LCC, where COT is assumed to be 10 ms. As shown in the example, any HARQ retransmission (e.g., HARQ Process IDs #0 and #2) is performed via LCC at least $n + 4$ subframe after receiving HARQ ACK/NACK feedback in subframe n. Only CCA on UCC for the initial transmission is necessary but the additional CCAs for the HARQ retransmissions are not necessary. It is due to the fact that regardless of occupying the UCC, the retransmissions are performed via the LCC where the transmitter can transmit data without any accessing the channel for the data transmission. Thus, it is applicable to the synchronous HARQ since we don't have to modify HARQ RTT in contrast to the HARQ retransmission via UCC in Sect. 3.1. In addition, the latency of HARQ retransmission is the same the legacy latency of HARQ retransmission. However, it may be overloaded in the LCC due to the data transmission in LCC and additional HARQ retransmission of UCC. Furthermore, the receiver shall monitor the LCC and UCC at the same.

3.3 HARQ Retransmission via One of Any Available LCC and UCC

Figure 5 shows an example of the HARQ retransmission via any available CC, where COT is assumed to be 10 ms. As shown in the example, HARQ retransmission of HARQ Process ID #2 is performed via LCC, and HARQ retransmission of HARQ process ID #0 is done via UCC. Compared to the HARQ retransmission via UCC in Sect. 3.1, HARQ RTT doesn't have to change and additional CCA may not be necessary for the HARQ retransmission. It is due to the fact

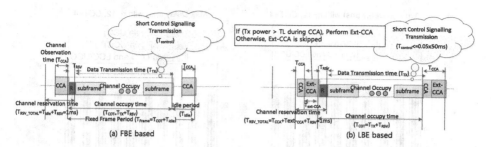

Fig. 6. Frame format for LBT operated in subframe boundary with reservation signal. (a) FBE and (b) LBE.

that whenever the UCC is available as a part of CCA of other data transmission, HARQ retransmission can also be performed in the UCC (e.g., HARQ Process ID #0). In contrast to the HARQ retransmission via LCC in Sect. 3.2, it is flexible since retransmission is up to scheduling policy when more than two CCs, where at least one of CCs is LCC, are available for HARQ retransmissions. It means that at least one CC, i.e., LCC, is available and it doesn't lead to performing CCA to access and occupy the UCC for the retransmission. Meanwhile, in addition, the traffic steering to the UCC can be achieved.

4   Performance Evaluation

4.1   Simulation Results

We compare the performance of proposed HARQ retransmissions in unlicensed spectrum, in terms of average delay and maximum delay. We also compare the proposed HARQ retransmission schemes in the view of what/how impact on the 3GPP LTE system.

For the simulation, we consider the total number of simulations is 10 times and the total number of trials is 100 trials for each simulation. We consider 4 BSs (i.e., eNBs) which perform CCA for data transmission in the same unlicensed carrier. We set the COTs to be 4 and 10 ms. We also set qs to be 12 and 26 for COT $= 4$ ms and 10 ms, respectively. Thus, when a BS occupies the UCC, the maximum allowed COT can be calculated, i.e., max COT $\leq 13/32 \times q$ for FBE based LBT and LBE based LBT (see Fig. 6 for frame format) [3]. In order to align the frame boundary, we assume that data is transmitted with subframe boundary after CCA and reservation signal, denoted by "R" in Fig. 6, may be included after CCA (including extended CCA for LBE) and before the subframe transmission. Thus, the total channel occupancy time, denonted by T_{COT}, for a BS when it occupies the channel after CCA can be calculated by $T_{COT} = T_{TX} + T_{RSV}$, where T_{TX} and T_{RSV} denote the data transmission time (i.e., the number of subframes) and time to transmit reservation signal, respectively. In addition, the channel reservation time, denoted by T_{RSV_TOTAL}, is in a unit of subframe, i.e., 1 ms. In particular, the total amount of channel reservation times for FBE

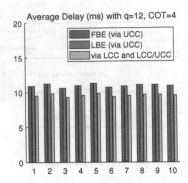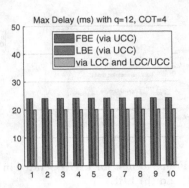

Fig. 7. (a) Average delay and (b) Maximum delay for HARQ retransmission of proposed schemes with $q = 12$ (COT = 4 ms).

and LBE are calculated by $T_{\text{RSV\_TOTAL}} = T_{\text{CCA}} + T_{\text{RSV}}$ and $T_{\text{RSV\_TOTAL}} = T_{\text{CCA}} + T_{\text{ext-CCA}} + T_{\text{RSV}}$, respectively. For the HARQ retransmission, we set the maximum number of retransmission trials to be 4 and frame error rate (FER) to 0.1.

Figures 7 and 8 show the average delay and maximum delay for HARQ retransmission schemes in unlicensed spectrum in Sect. 3, with $q = 12$ (i.e., COT = 4 ms) and $q = 26$ (i.e., COT = 10 ms), respectively. (i) Latency of HARQ retransmission via UCC is longer than that of HARQ retransmission via LCC and LCC/UCC (i.e., any one of available CCs), relatively. It is due to the fact that additional CCA for the HARQ retransmission may be necessary for the HARQ retransmission via UCC. However, those additional CCAs for the HARQ retransmission is not necessary for the HARQ retransmission via LCC and LCC/UCC since the transmitter can access any available CC either LCC or UCC. (ii) Delay in the larger value of q is much longer than that in the small value of q, relatively. It implies that a larger value of COT makes the system worse because if a station occupies the channel, the other (needs to perform HARQ retransmission in the UCC) shall wait till the COT expires or till the channel is available (i.e., idle).

4.2   Comparison of HARQ Retransmission Techniques

Table 1 summaries the comparisons of the proposed HARQ retransmissions via UCC, via LCC, and via any available CC (i.e., either LCC or UCC). As shown in Table 1, HARQ retransmissions via UCC do not impact the current 3GPP LTE [1], but latency due to the retransmission increases when the COT exceeds the HARQ RTT. It is due to the fact that additional CCA is necessary to occupy the UCC, which is the same CC as that for the initial transmission. Otherwise, the transmission is dropped and the transmitter shall re-initialise data transmission. In addition, as shown in Figs. 7 and 8, the average delay and maximum delay for HARQ retransmissions via LCC and via any available CC are shorter than those for HARQ retransmissions via UCC, relatively. It is due to the fact

Table 1. Comparison of HARQ retransmission schemes.

	Via UCC	Via LCC	Via LCC/UCC
What/How	- HARQ Retransmissions via the same carrier (UCC) as the carrier for initial transmission	-HARQ Retransmissions via LCC	-HARQ Retransmissions via one of any available LCC and UCC
Pros	- Same (or similar) legacy approach	- No additional CCA	- No additional CCA
	- Applicable to any scheduling (cross-carrier and self-carrier scheduling)	- Same (or similar) HARQ performance (RTT timer, latency of retransmission)	- Same (or similar) HARQ performance (RTT timer, latency of retransmission)
Cons	- Additional CCA is necessary (due to regulatory requirements)	- Overhead in LCC due to retransmission and initial transmissions	- May be overhead in LCC due to retransmissions and initial transmissions
	- Relatively long latency	- HARQ channel ID mapping and relevant operation is necessary	- HARQ channel ID mapping and relevant operation is necessary for the retransmission via LCC
DL PHY control impact	- No impact	- UE monitors UCC (for initial transmissions) and LCC (for retransmissions)	- UE monitors UCC (for initial transmissions) and LCC/UCC (for retransmissions)
		- DCI needs to be modified for HARQ channel mapping	- DCI needs to be modified for HARQ channel mapping
HARQ impact	- Timing for retransmission may be longer due to CCA and limited COT	- No change on HARQ timing	- No change on HARQ timing
	- No impact on HARQ Processing ID	- HARQ channel ID mapping and relevant operation is necessary	- HARQ channel ID mapping and relevant operation is necessary
Impact on LBT (FBE)	- UCC shall be occupied for retransmissions. Otherwise, latency increases due to Fixed Frame Period	- No impact since CCA is only necessary for the initial transmission	- No impact since CCA is only necessary for the initial transmission, but CCA is only necessary for the retransmission via UCC
Impact on LBT (LBE)	- UCC shall be occupied for retransmissions. Otherwise, latency increases due to additional CCA	- No impact since CCA is only necessary for the initial transmission	- No impact since CCA is only necessary for the initial transmission, but CCA is only necessary for the retransmission via UCC

that the LBT time for the retransmissions is unnecessary since the transmitter can retransmit the data via CC, which is always available without accessing the channel for retransmissions. However, additional modifications related to HARQ processing such as distinguishing method between the retransmission and other transmissions in the occupied CC and indicating the CC which is used for the initial transmission. Nevertheless, it is clear that latency of data transmission due to additional CCA of the system operating in unlicensed spectrum band decreases.

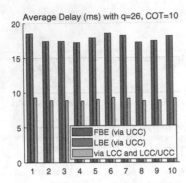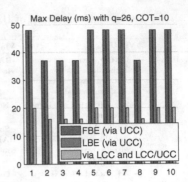

Fig. 8. (a) Average delay and (b) Maximum delay for HARQ retransmission of proposed schemes with $q = 26$ (COT $= 10$ ms).

5   Conclusion

In this paper, taking into account the regulatory requirements in the unlicensed spectrum such as CCA, we propose new HARQ retransmission techniques in unlicensed spectrum, i.e., HARQ retransmission via UCC, HARQ retransmission via LCC, and HARQ retransmission via any available CC. Although all proposed HARQ retransmission techniques in the unlicensed spectrum need to modify the current system, i.e., LTE, those algorithms are applicable to the retransmission in the unlicensed spectrum. In particular, proposed HARQ retransmission via LCC and via any available CC attain high performance in terms of transmission time. In addition, the proposed algorithms and further extensions taking into account regulatory requirements in the unlicensed spectrum can be used in the uplink service and in the coexistence of downlink and uplink service.

References

1. Evolved Universal Terrestrial Radio Access (E-UTRA) and Evolved Universal Terrestrial Radio Access Network (E-UTRAN); Overall description, Stage 2. 3GPP TS 36.300
2. Evolved Universal Terrestrial Radio Access (E-UTRA), Physical layer procedures. 3GPP TS 36.213
3. Harmonized European Standard, Broadband Radio Access Networks (BRAN), 5 GHz high performance RLAN. ETSI EN 301 893
4. IEEE Standard for Information Technology-Telecommunications and Information Exchange between Systems - Local and Metropolitan Area Networks-Specific Requirements - Part 11: Wireless LAN Medium Access Control (MAC) and Physical Layer (PHY) Specifications. IEEE 802.11-2020
5. NR; NR and NG-RAN Overall description; Stage-2. 3GPP TS 38.300
6. Physical layer procedures for shared spectrum channel access. 3GPP TS 37.213
7. Study on NR-based access to unlicensed spectrum. 3GPP TR 38.889
8. Cisco Annual Internet Report (2018–2023) White Paper. CISCO (2020)

9. Ahmadi, S.: 5G NR: Architecture, Technology, Implementation, and Operation of 3GPP New Radio Standards. Wiley, Hoboken (2019)
10. Chen, B., Chen, J., Gao, Y., Zhang, J.: Coexistence of LTE-LAA and WI-FI on 5 GHZ with corresponding deployment scenarios: a survey. IEEE Communic. Surv. Tutor. **19**(1), 7–32 (2017). https://doi.org/10.1109/COMST.2016.2593666
11. Dahlman, E., et al.: 5G Wireless access: requirements and realization. IEEE Commun. Mag. **52**(12), 42–47 (2014). https://doi.org/10.1109/MCOM.2014.6979985
12. Kim, E., Lee, Y., Heesoo, L.: An applicable repeated transmission for low latency and reliable services. IEEE Trans. Veh. Technol. **69**(8), 8468–8482 (2020). https://doi.org/10.1109/TVT.2020.2995846

Beneficial Online Price Coordination in the O2O Era Added Mobile Channel

Yang Bai[1] and Wenqi Song[2(✉)]

[1] Business School, Shandong University of Technology, Zibo 255000, China
[2] Department of Ophthalmology, Zibo Central Hospital, Zibo 255000, China
s930032151@163.com

Abstract. This paper proposes an innovative pricing discount cooperative strategy in an O2O era adds a mobile channel, and models the market share into three consumer bases: one prefers buying the products in stores, one prefers shopping online, and one prefers buying products using a mobile App. In the O2O added mobile channel (O2O&M), the competition promotes the manufacturer aggressively set a higher selling and wholesale price, resulting in the retailer increasing his selling price. Surprisingly, this allows the manufacturer to direct online mobile and computer channels to gain more profits and achieve Pareto-improving. Meanwhile, the manufacturer utilizes the online computer channel price discount contract as an effective mechanism to improve their respective profits.

Keywords: O2O&M supply chain · Price discount contracts · Channel coordination

1 Introduction

With the rapid growth of technologies, online shopping has significantly changed our purchase patterns over the past decades. As the New York Times reported, more than half of top suppliers began to use online technology to sell directly to consumers through the internet and mobile devices. More and more companies realize that online technologies help them reduce margin costs and expand the consumer market, ultimately promoting the whole channel's sales and increasing their profits.

Recently, with the development of online technology, a large number of manufacturers (or suppliers) such as IBM. P&G, McDonald's, and HP are involved in introducing mobile orders to redesign their supply chain channels [1–3]. When the manufacturers (or suppliers) open a newly added mobile channel, they may attract the customers who prefer buying the products in stores through the traditional channel, and capture the customers who prefer shopping online through the direct online channel, also could attract young customers who prefer buying products use mobile App through the mobile channel. However, the benefit of expanding market segments also leads to a disadvantage of channel conflict. When the manufacturers (or suppliers) open an online computer and mobile channels, they would take away some market share from the traditional channel and compete with retailers. Retailers have no choice except to reduce the price to attract

B.-Y. Chang and C. Choi (Eds.): AsiaSim 2021, CCIS 1636, pp. 86–99, 2022.
https://doi.org/10.1007/978-981-19-6857-0_9

consumers. Although this competition may lead to conflict, they may not be worse off, and it is unwise to boycott the online channel and drive customers to buy elsewhere [4].

In this paper, we consider pricing discount decisions in an O2O era and added a mobile channel (O2O&M) supply chain channel. In our research, we propose an innovative pricing discount cooperative strategy in an O2O&M channel and model the market share into three consumer bases: one prefers buying the products in stores, one prefers shopping online, and one prefers buying products using a mobile App. The main contributions of this paper are: will fill up the supply chain pricing discount decision literature stream of the manufacturers directing traditional retailer channel, online channel, and mobile channel together. This paper addresses some main research questions:

1) What optimal pricing policies for traditional, online, and mobile channels?
2) How does pricing discount contracts promotion strategy impact the whole supply chain?
3) Does pricing discount contracts improves channel profits and reduce conflict?

The rest of this paper is organized as follows. Section 2 surveys the pertinent literature, and Sect. 3 derives the pricing discount contract models in an O2O&M channel supply chain. Section 4 compares the main results derived from O2O&M channel. Section 5 offers our conclusions and future research.

2 Literature Review

2.1 Mobile Channel

Bang et al. (2014) develop a theoretical framework for understanding the interactions between mobile and traditional online channels for products with different characteristics. Huang et al. [6] use empirical analysis to indicate that adopting the mobile channel will promote channel conflict. However, the consumers' purchases increased overall. Kim and Baek [7] proposed a structural model to investigate why consumers use mobile app channels. They show that time convenience, interactivity, and compatibility positively influenced the demand for mobile channels. Yin et al. [8] Compare the traditional recommendation model and location-based mobile marketing recommendation model in the mobile channel. Gao et al. [9] investigate the effectiveness of the mobile online channel. Amrouche et al. [10] study the noon-cooperation and cooperation strategies in the O2O&M channel supply chain. They find that manufacturers will try to impose a revenue-sharing strategy to benefit the whole channel. However, different from the above studies' research on recommendation models using empirical analysis, this paper set a game-theoretic model to illustrate the effect of pricing discount contracts to the channel members' profits in the O2O&M channel.

2.2 Coordination Incentive Mechanisms

Numerous contributions have been made to channel price strategy coordination mechanisms. Dada and Srikanth [11] formulated a pricing model under quantity discounts.

Winter [12] and Iyer [13] utilized multi-echelon coordination mechanisms to show us that linear price contracts and quantity discounts contracts will not be sufficient. Chiang et al. [1] study a pricing-setting model to show us that online channels are not always detrimental to the retailer. Cachon [14] showed that profit sharing and quantity discounts could coordinate a supply chain when price strategy mechanisms are involved. Yao et al. [15] utilized Bertrand and Stackelberg models and looked at price competition in a dual channel. Kurata et al. [16] illustrated an optimal pricing decision for brand and channel competition. Huang and Swaminathan [17] considered four different pricing strategies in dual channels. Chen et al. [18] found that price and quality decisions may increase the profit of the dual-channel for both retailers and manufacturers. The above research studies on coordination incentive mechanisms focus on selling incentive contracts. They didn't focus on different price discount incentive contracts in the O2O&M channel supply chain.

2.3 Price Differentiation

Boyaci and Ray [19] investigate the differences in immediate and dynamic effects of promotional and regular prices on sales. Haucap and Heimeshoff [20] explore how consumers react toward price differentiation between on-net and off-net calls in mobile telecommunications. Herbon [21] develop an optimization model with price differentiation over time. They show us that the price differentiation strategy may mitigate the retailer's risk of falling in the process of implementing price discrimination. Danzon [22] uses the differential pricing theory to incorporate insurance coverage and address static and dynamic efficiency. Raza and Govindaluri [23] investigate the mathematical models for single-channel coordination that integrate price differentiation for green and regular products. The models provide comprehensive decision support to determine important decision differentiation prices. The key difference between this study and the above studies is that we investigate the different price decisions in the mobile channel.

3 Models

This paper considers the price decision strategy of manufacturers directing the O2O&M supply chain. Chiang et al. [1] and Yan et al. [2] show that most products are less acceptable from web-based channels than the traditional channel. If customers buy the product from an online store, they should typically have to wait several days for delivery and be charged a shipping and handling fee [24]. Second, it is difficult to eliminate the production uncertainty completely only after viewing the photographs on the web page. Even the customer can refund the product but has to pay the delivery fee, and the refund is typically only partial, reducing the customer's consumption value [25]. Third, as Yan et al. [2] addressed, the online seller may be located in another city. Therefore, the after-sale service questions arise. As a result, the demand functions are assumed to be linear in price and cross-price effect, and the demand functions can be addressed as

$$D_1 = g(1 + \gamma) - \beta p_1 + \mu p_2 \tag{1}$$

$$D_2 = (1 - g) - \beta p_2 + \mu p_1 \tag{2}$$

Here, D_1 is the online demand and D_2 is the offline demand. The percentage of consumers going to the offline channel is $0 < g < 1$. On the other hand, $1 - g$ is the percentage of consumer goes to the online channel. The online mobile channel baseline demand is noted as γ. In order to save notions, we assume $g = \frac{\theta}{2}$, where θ is the product compatibility. Therefore, the demand functions can be expressed as

$$D_1 = \frac{\theta}{2} - p_1 + \theta p_2 \tag{3}$$

$$D_2 = \left(1 - \frac{\theta}{2}\right) - p_2 + \theta p_1 + \theta p_3 \tag{4}$$

$$D_3 = \frac{\theta \gamma}{2} - p_3 + \theta p_2 \tag{5}$$

Here, D_1 is the online computer channel demand, D_2 is the offline traditional retailer demand, and D_3 is the online mobile channel demand.

3.1 O2O&M Supply Chain

3.1.1 Mobile and Computer with a Noon-Different Price

In this part, we compare the manufacturers directing the O2O supply chain and the O2O&M supply chain. In this scenario, we assume the online computer channel and mobile channel have the same price decisions, which means, $p_1 = p_3$. The demands functions can be expressed as

$$D_1 = \frac{\theta}{2}(1 + \gamma) - p_1 + \theta p_2 \tag{6}$$

$$D_2 = \left(1 - \frac{\theta}{2}\right) - p_2 + \theta p_1 \tag{7}$$

The expected profit function of the manufacturer and retailer can be expressed as follows

$$\pi_M = p_1 D_1 + \omega D_2 \tag{8}$$

$$\pi_R = (p_2 - \omega) D_2 \tag{9}$$

3.1.2 Mobile and Computer with Different Price

In this scenario, we assume the online computer channel and mobile channel have the same price decisions, which means, $p_1 \neq p_3$. The demands functions can be expressed as

$$D_1 = \frac{\theta}{2} - p_1 + \theta p_2 \tag{10}$$

$$D_2 = \left(1 - \frac{\theta}{2}\right) - p_2 + \theta p_1 + \theta p_3 \tag{11}$$

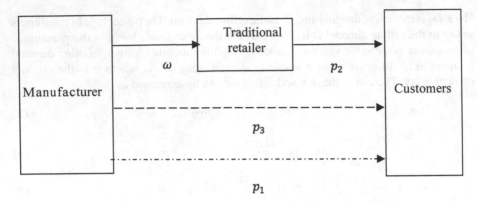

Retailer channel ———▶ Computer channel ·····▶ Mobile channel ――▶

Fig. 1. The O2O&M channel distribution diagram.

$$D_3 = \frac{\theta\gamma}{2} - p_3 + \theta p_2 \tag{12}$$

The expected profit function of the manufacturer and retailer can be expressed as follows (Fig. 1)

$$\pi_M = p_1 D_1 + p_3 D_3 + \omega D_2 \tag{13}$$

$$\pi_R = (p_2 - \omega) D_2 \tag{14}$$

Lemma 1. In the O2O&M channel and noon-added mobile supply chain, the optimal pricing strategies and profits for the online and the traditional retailer are summarized in Table 1.

The outcomes in Lemma 1 show that the online prices and manufacturer profits are significantly affected by the O2O&M channel. In the traditional retailer channel, the optimal decisions for both the manufacturer and the traditional retailer are influenced by the differential of return policies. The traditional offline retailer's demand and profits are the same from the newly added or noon-added mobile channel strategies.

Proposition 1. Comparison of different ω, p, D, and π.

1) $\omega^{ADP} > \omega^{AOP} > \omega^{NAM}$;
2) $p_1^{ADP} > p_1^{AOP} > p_1^{NAM}$, $p_2^{ADP} > p_2^{AOP} > p_2^{NAM}$;
3) $D_{ON}^{ADP} > D_{ON}^{AOP} > D_{ON}^{NAM}$, $D_{OF}^{ADP} = D_{OF}^{AOP} = D_{OF}^{NAM}$;
4) $\pi_M^{ADP} > \pi_M^{AOP} > \pi_M^{NAM}$, $\pi_R^{ADP} > \pi_R^{AOP} > \pi_R^{NAM}$.

In the O2O&M channel, the competition promotes manufacturers aggressively setting higher selling and wholesale price, resulting in the retailer increasing his selling price. Surprisingly, this situation allows both the manufacture directing online mobile

Table 1. The equilibrium outcomes of the O2O era added and noon-added mobile channel Scenarios

	Added mobile channel		Noon-added mobile channel
	OP	DP	
ω	$\dfrac{2-\theta+(1+\gamma)\theta^2}{4-4\theta^2}$	$\dfrac{2-\theta+(1+\gamma)\theta^2}{4-8\theta^2}$	$\dfrac{2-\theta+\theta^2}{4(1-\theta^2)}$
p_1	$\dfrac{\theta(3+\gamma-\theta)}{4(1-\theta^2)}$	$\dfrac{\theta[3-\theta(1+\theta-\gamma\theta)]}{4-8\theta^2}$	$\dfrac{3\theta-\theta^2}{4(1-\theta^2)}$
p_2	$\dfrac{6-\theta(3-2\gamma\theta-\theta^2)}{8-8\theta^2}$	$\dfrac{6-\theta[3+2\theta(1-\gamma-\theta)]}{8-16\theta^2}$	$\dfrac{6-3\theta+\theta^3}{8-8\theta^2}$
p_3		$\dfrac{\theta\left[2+\gamma-\theta+(1-\gamma)\theta^2\right]}{4-8\theta^2}$	
D_1	$\dfrac{(4+2\gamma-\theta)\theta}{8}$	$\dfrac{(4-\theta)\theta}{8}$	$\dfrac{(4-\theta)\theta}{8}$
D_2	$\dfrac{2-\theta}{8}$	$\dfrac{2-\theta}{8}$	$\dfrac{2-\theta}{8}$
D_3		$\dfrac{(2+2\gamma-\theta)\theta}{8}$	
π_R	$\dfrac{(2-\theta)^2}{64}$	$\dfrac{(2-\theta)^2}{64}$	$\dfrac{(2-\theta)^2}{64}$
π_M	$\dfrac{4-\theta\left[4-\theta\left\{\begin{array}{c}15+2\gamma(6+\gamma)\\-8\theta-4\gamma\theta+\theta^2\end{array}\right\}\right]}{32(1-\theta^2)}$	$\dfrac{4-\theta\left[\begin{array}{c}4-\{19+2\gamma(4+\gamma)\}\theta\\+4(3+\gamma)\theta^2-2(2-\gamma)\gamma\theta^3\end{array}\right]}{32-64\theta^2}$	$\dfrac{4-\theta[4-(5-\theta)(3-\theta)\theta]}{32(1-\theta^2)}$

and computer channels to gain more profits and achieve Pareto-improving. Additionally, there is no impact on the traditional offline retailer's demand, even increasing his selling price. This means the traditional offline retailer may also benefit from such an O2O&M channel.

Proposition 2. (Impact of θ on ω^{ADP}, p^{ADP}, and D^{ADP})

(1) ω^{ADP} is decreasing in θ, given $\theta \in \left(0, 3+\gamma - \sqrt{8+6\gamma+\gamma^2}\right)$. Otherwise ω^{AM} is increasing in θ, given $\theta \in \left(3+\gamma - \sqrt{8+6\gamma+\gamma^2}, 1\right)$; ω^{NAM} is decreasing in θ, given $\theta \in (0, 3-2\sqrt{2})$. Otherwise ω^{NAM} is increasing in θ, given $\theta \in \left(3-2\sqrt{2}, 1\right)$.

(2) p_1^{ADP} and p_3^{ADP} are increasing in θ; p_2^{ADP} is first decreasing and then increasing in θ.

(3) D_1^{ADP} and D_3^{ADP} are increasing in θ, D_2^{ADP} is decreasing in θ.

Proposition 2 shows that in the O2O&M channel, the manufacturer's wholesale price changes with product compatibility θ. When θ is high, the manufacturer sets a higher wholesale price, and the manufacturer sets a lower wholesale price when θ is low. This which means when θ is low, the product compatibility with traditional offline retailer sales is larger, and consumers will transfer the products to the offline channel, in order to keep the demand from the offline retailer, the manufacturer sets a lower wholesale price. On the other hand, as the product compatibility parameter θ increase, there is no difference between customers buying the products offline or online. Because of the convenience of online channels, a plenty number of customers transfer to the online channel from the offline channel, and the manufacturer aggressively sets a high wholesale price to the retailer, which decreases the offline demand.

On the other hand, as the wholesale price decrease, the offline retailer would like to set a low sell price. However, as the manufacturer sets a high wholesale price, the retailer has to increase its sell price to recoup the loss without affecting sales. Meanwhile, online mobile and computer channel demands are still increasing even though online channels are increasing their prices. Additionally, as the traditional offline retailer decrease its price, the demand for offline channel is the same from both of the newly added or noon-added mobile channel strategies.

4   Coordination with Price Discount Contracts

This section investigates different price discount contracts (Online computer channel price discount contract, online mobile channel price discount contract and offline retailer channel price discount contract) in the O2O&M channel. We compare the different price discount contracts and determine which contract could help all channel members gain more profits and achieve Pareto-improving.

4.1   Online Computer Channel Price Discount Contract

In this scenario, the manufacturer utilizes a price discount contract as an effective mechanism in the online computer channel to check whether this strategy is beneficial. In this section, we assume the wholesale price $\omega^{ACD} = \theta p_1^{ACD}$. Therefore, the profit functions of manufacturer and retailer can be written as follows:

$$\pi_R^{ACD} = \left(p_2^{ACD} - \theta p_1^{ACD}\right) D_2^{ACD} \tag{15}$$

$$\pi_M^{ACD} = p_1^{ACD} D_1^{ACD} + p_3^{ACD} D_3^{ACD} + \theta p_1^{ACD} D_2^{ACD} \tag{16}$$

4.2   Online Mobile Channel Price Discount Contract

In this scenario, the manufacturer utilizes a price discount contract as an effective mechanism in the online mobile channel to check whether this strategy is beneficial. In this section, we assume the wholesale price $\omega^{AMD} = \theta p_3^{AMD}$. Therefore, the profit functions of manufacturer and retailer can be written as follows:

$$\pi_R^{AMD} = (p_2^{AMD} - \theta p_3^{AMD}) D_2^{AMD} \tag{17}$$

$$\pi_M^{AMD} = p_1^{AMD} D_1^{AMD} + p_3^{AMD} D_3^{AMD} + \theta p_3^{AMD} D_2^{AMD} \tag{18}$$

4.3 Offline Traditional Retailer Price Discount Contract

In this scenario, the manufacturer utilizes a price discount contract as an effective mechanism in the online mobile channel to check whether this strategy benefits. In this section, we assume the wholesale price $\omega^{ATD} = \theta p_2^{ATD}$. Therefore, the profit functions of manufacturer and retailer can be written as follows:

$$\pi_R^{ATD} = (p_2^{ATD} - \theta p_2^{ATD})D_2^{ATD} \tag{19}$$

$$\pi_M^{ATD} = p_1^{ATD}D_1^{ATD} + p_3^{ATD}D_3^{ATD} + \theta p_2^{ATD}D_2^{ATD} \tag{20}$$

Based on the profit functions, the equilibrium outcomes of the three price discount scenarios are summarized in Table 2.

Table 2. Equilibrium outcomes of the three price discount scenarios

	Online channel price discount contracts		Offline channel price discount contract
	Computer channel	Mobile channel	
ω	$\frac{\theta^2[-6+\theta(2+\theta-2\gamma\theta)]}{4(-2+3\theta^2+\theta^4)}$	$\frac{\theta^2\left[\begin{array}{c}-2(2+\gamma)\\+2\theta+(-2+\gamma)\theta^2\end{array}\right]}{4(-2+3\theta^2+\theta^4)}$	$\frac{4\theta-\theta^2[2-\theta(-1+\gamma+\theta)]}{8-4\theta^2(2+\theta)}$
p_1	$\frac{\theta[-6+\theta(2+\theta-2\gamma\theta)]}{4(-2+3\theta^2+\theta^4)}$	$\frac{\theta(-4+\theta-2\gamma\theta^2+\theta^3)}{4(-2+3\theta^2+\theta^4)}$	$\frac{8\theta+\theta^2\left[2-\theta\left\{\begin{array}{c}4+\theta\\-\gamma(2+\theta)\end{array}\right\}\right]}{8[2-\theta^2(2+\theta)]}$
p_2	$-\frac{8-\theta\left[4-\theta\left\{\begin{array}{c}2+(1-\theta)^2\theta\\+2\gamma(1+\theta^2)\end{array}\right\}\right]}{8(-2+3\theta^2+\theta^4)}$	$\frac{8+\theta(-4+4\gamma\theta+\theta^2+\theta^4)}{8(-2+3\theta^2+\theta^4)}$	$\frac{-4+\theta[2-\theta(-1+\gamma+\theta)]}{-8+4\theta^2(2+\theta)}$
p_3	$\frac{\theta\left[\begin{array}{c}-2(1+\gamma)+\theta\\2(2-\gamma)\theta^2+\theta^3\end{array}\right]}{4(-2+3\theta^2+\theta^4)}$	$\frac{\theta\left[\begin{array}{c}-2(2+\gamma)\\+2\theta-(2-\gamma)\theta^2\end{array}\right]}{4(-2+3\theta^2+\theta^4)}$	$\frac{\theta\left[\begin{array}{c}-4-\theta(2+\theta^2)\\+\gamma\{-4+\theta^2(2+\theta)\}\end{array}\right]}{8[2-\theta^2(2+\theta)]}$
D_1	$-\frac{\theta\left[\begin{array}{c}4-2(4+\gamma)\theta^2+\theta^3\\-2(3-\gamma)\theta^4+\theta^5\end{array}\right]}{8(-2+3\theta^2+\theta^4)}$	$\frac{(4-\theta)\theta}{8}$	$\frac{\theta[8-\theta\{6+\theta(6+\theta+\gamma\theta)\}]}{8[2-\theta^2(2+\theta)]}$
D_2	$-\frac{8+\theta\left[\begin{array}{c}-4-2(5-\gamma)\theta\\+5\theta^2-2\gamma\theta^3+\theta^4\end{array}\right]}{8(-2+3\theta^2+\theta^4)}$	$-\frac{8+\theta\left[\begin{array}{c}-4-8\theta\\+\theta^2\{5+\theta(-4+2\gamma+\theta)\}\end{array}\right]}{8(-2+3\theta^2+\theta^4)}$	$\frac{-4+\theta[2-\theta(-1+\gamma+\theta)]}{-8+4\theta^2(2+\theta)}$

(continued)

Table 2. (*continued*)

Online channel price discount contracts		Offline channel price discount contract
Computer channel	Mobile channel	
D_3 $\frac{(2+2\gamma-\theta)\theta}{8}$	$\dfrac{\gamma\left(-4\theta+6\theta^3+4\theta^5\right)-\theta^3(-4+\theta+\theta^3)}{8(-2+3\theta^2+\theta^4)}$	$\dfrac{\gamma\theta\left[-4+\theta^2(4+3\theta)\right]-\theta[(2+\theta)(2-(4-\theta)\theta)]}{8[-2+\theta^2(2+\theta)]}$

Proposition 3. Impact of θ on ω, p, and D using different price discount contracts.

(1) When $\theta < \theta'$, ω^{ACD}, ω^{AMD}, and ω^{ATD} are increasing in θ;
(2) $p_1^{ACD}, p_2^{ACD}, p_3^{ACD}, p_1^{ATD}, p_2^{ATD}$, and p_3^{ATD} are increasing in θ. p_1^{AMD}, p_2^{AMD}, and p_3^{AMD} are first decreasing and then increasing in θ;
(3) D_1^{ACD}, D_1^{ATD}, and D_3^{ATD} are first increasing and then decreasing in θ. D_2^{ACD}, D_2^{AMD}, and D_2^{ATD} are first decreasing and then increasing in θ; D_3^{ACD}, D_1^{AMD}, and D_3^{AMD} are increasing in θ. Meanwhile, D_3^{AMD} is significantly decreasing in γ.

Proposition 3 shows that when the product compatibility θ is low, no one will buy from the online channel, in order to keep the demand from the offline retailer, the manufacturer sets a lower wholesale price to the offline retailer. As θ increases, consumers are transferred to the online channel from offline channel, increasing the demand for the online computer channel and decreasing the offline channel, and promoting the manufacturer to increase his wholesale price to dig more profits. All selling prices are increasing with θ under online computer channels or offline channel price discount contracts. At first, when θ, the online channels set a lower price to attract more consumers. As θ increases, consumers transfer from offline to online in order to get more profits without loss demands, and the online members increase their selling prices. Meanwhile, as the manufacturer increases his whole sale price, the offline retailer also increases his selling price. Additionally, when the manufacturer newly added a mobile channel, as θ increases, the consumers first transfer to the online computer channel. In order competitive with online computer channels, the online mobile channel set a lower selling price. However, as the online channels attract more consumers, the online mobile channel increases its selling price to get more profits. Meanwhile, as the consumers first transfer to the online channels, this gives offline retailers stress to decrease their selling prices to attract more consumers. Moreover, a higher wholesale price incentives the retailer to increase his selling price (Fig. 2, 3, 4 and 5). On the other hand, higher online selling prices will decrease some online demands and increase some offline demands.

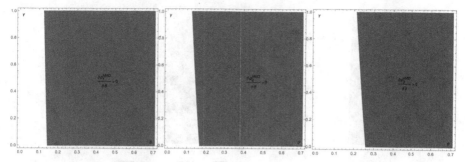

Fig. 2. Effect of θ on p_1^{AMD}, p_2^{AMD}, and p_3^{AMD}

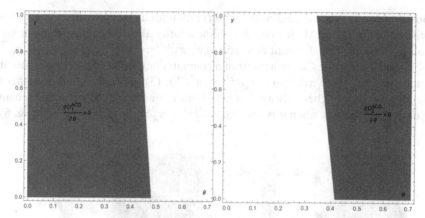

Fig. 3. Effect of θ on D_1^{ACD} and D_2^{ACD}

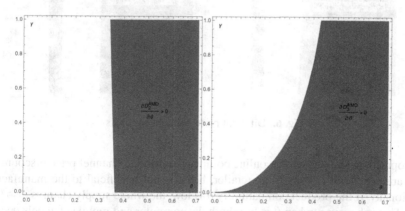

Fig. 4. Effect of θ on D_2^{AMD} and D_3^{AMD}

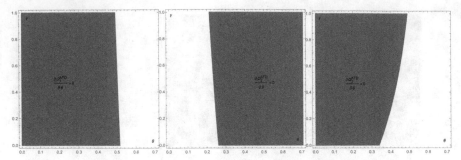

Fig. 5. Effect of θ on D_1^{ATD}, D_2^{ATD}, and D_3^{ATD}

Proposition 4. (1) When the online computer or mobile channel price discount contracts are utilized in the O2O&M channel, the offline retailer always benefits from computer or mobile channel price discount contracts (i.e., $\pi_R^{ACD} > \pi_R^{ADP}$ and $\pi_R^{AMD} > \pi_R^{ADP}$); (2) the manufacturer does not benefit from a computer or mobile channel price discount contract; (i.e., $\pi_M^{ACD} < \pi_M^{ADP}$ and $\pi_M^{AMD} < \pi_M^{ADP}$); (3) under the condition, that the whole channel supply chain always benefits from online computer or mobile channel price discount contracts when θ is low (i.e., $\pi_M^{ACD} + \pi_R^{ACD} > \pi_M^{ADP} + \pi_R^{ADP}$) (Fig. 6).

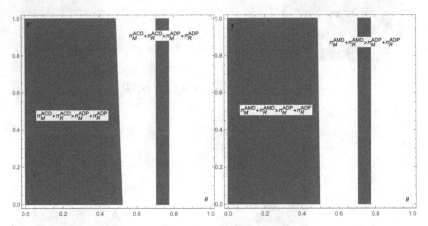

Fig. 6. Different price discount contracts

Proposition 4 indicates that online computer or mobile channel price discount contracts are beneficial to the offline retailer, but it is not beneficial to the manufacturer. Additionally, if the product compatibility θ is low, the whole supply chain is also beneficial. That is because, when θ is low, both the computer and mobile channels decrease their selling price to attract more consumers. In this situation, if the manufacturer utilizes an online computer or mobile channel price discount contract, this strategy will set a lower wholesale price and incentivize the retailer to set a lower selling price and ultimately increase the profits of the retailer channel. Meanwhile, as the profits of the offline retailer channel increase, it will recoup the online channel's losses, which ultimately leads to a higher profit for the whole supply chain. As a result, through online computer or mobile channel price discount contract, both the manufacturer and retailer can achieve a Pareto-improving if and only if the product compatibility θ is not high. Therefore, when the product compatibility is not high, the manufacturer can use the online price discount contract as effective mechanisms to improve their profits.

Corollary 1. (1) The manufacturer always benefits more from an online computer channel price discount contract (i.e., $\pi_M^{ACD} > \pi_M^{AMD}$); (2) the offline retailer always benefits less from online computer channel price discount contracts (i.e., $\pi_R^{ACD} < \pi_R^{AMD}$); (3) under the condition of $0 < \theta < \frac{\sqrt{2}}{2}$, the whole channel supply chain always bene­fits more from online computer channel price discount contract when θ is low (i.e., $\pi_M^{ACD} + \pi_R^{ACD} > \pi_M^{AMD} + \pi_R^{AMD}$).

Corollary 1 reveals that compare with an online mobile channel price discount contract, an online computer channel price discount contract is always beneficial to the manufacturer. And less beneficial to the retailer. Meanwhile, it is always more beneficial to the whole channel. That's because the product compatibility θ should be much lower in the online mobile channel price discount contract than in the online computer price discount contract. This incentive the online channel members to decrease their selling prices and lead the manufacturer to set a lower wholesale price, ultimate promotion the retailer to decrease his selling price. Which helps the offline retailer attract more consumers. However, the increased profit for the manufacturer and whole channel supply chain is much more than the loss of the offline retailer. Therefore, the manufacturer utilizes the online computer channel price discount contract as an effective mechanism to improve their respective profits.

Proposition 5. (1) When a traditional offline retailer price discount contract is utilized in the O2O&M channel, the offline retailer always benefits from this strategy, but less benefits than online channel price discount contracts (i.e., $\pi_R^{AMD} > \pi_R^{ACD} > \pi_R^{ATD} > \pi_R^{ADP}$); (2) the manufacturer does not benefit from traditional offline retailer price discount contracts but benefits from online channel price discount contracts; (i.e., $\pi_M^{ADP} > \pi_M^{ATD} > \pi_M^{ACD}$); (3) under the condition of $0 < \theta < \sqrt{2}/2$, compared with the online channel price discount contracts, the whole channel supply chain does not benefit from offline channel price discount contracts but always benefits from than baseline model when θ is low (i.e., $\pi_M^{ACD} + \pi_R^{ACD} > \pi_M^{AMD} + \pi_R^{AMD} > \pi_M^{ATD} + \pi_R^{ATD} > \pi_M^{ADP} + \pi_R^{ADP}$).

Proposition 5 shows us that both the online channel and offline channel price discount contracts can achieve more profits when the product compatibility θ is not very high. In addition, the online computer channel price discount contract is the most effective incentive mechanism to improve both the manufacturer and retailer to achieve Pareto results.

5 Conclusions

This paper considers pricing discount decisions in an O2O&M supply chain. Following the analytical observations derived from our O2O&M model, we present that when the product compatibility θ is not very high, the newly added mobile channel can help the whole channel achieve the Pareto improvement. Therefore, it is suggested that the manufacturer should seek an online mobile channel cooperation mechanism. Meanwhile, all the channel members benefit from the online computer channel price discount contract. Consequently, valuable managerial insights to business managers are that channel directors should invest more money to redesign their online channel and cooperate with competitive channel members to get more performance.

Due to the limitation of this research, we suggest some extensions for future study. First, we can link the recommendation model with our O2O&M model to investigate online consumers' purchase stickiness. Second, other incentive contracts can also be used in our model. Third, the pricing decisions should change with time, which also needs to consider the dynamic pricing decisions.

Conflicts of Interest. The authors declare that they have no conflicts of interest regarding this work.

Funding. This research was funded by the National Social Science Foundation of China (Grant No.21CGL050).

Data Availability. The experimental data used to support the findings of this study are available from the corresponding author upon request.

References

1. Chiang,W.K., Chhajed, D., Hess, J.D.: Direct marketing, indirect profits: a strategic analysis of dual-channel supply-chain design. Manage. Sci. **49**, 1–20 (2003). https://doi.org/10.1287/mnsc491112749
2. Yan, R., Cao, Z., Pei, Z.: Manufacturer's cooperative advertising, demand uncertainty, and information sharing. J. Bus. Res. **69**, 709–717 (2016)
3. Gao, F., Su, X.: Omnichannel retail operations with buy-online-and-pick-up-in-store. Mamage. Sci. **63**, 2478–2492 (2016). https://doi.org/10.1287/mnsc20162473
4. Hua, G., Wang, S., Cheng, T.C.E.: Price and lead time decisions in dual-channel supply chains. Eur. J. Oper. Res. **205**, 113–126 (2010)
5. Bang, Y., Lee, D.-J., Han, K., Hwang, M., Ahn, J.-H.: Channel capabilities, product characteristics, and the impacts of mobile channel introduction. J. Manage. Inf. Systg. **30**, 101–126 (2014). https://doi.org/10.2753/MIS0742-1222300204
6. Huang, X., Gu, J.W., Ching, W.K., Siu, T.K.: Impact of secondary market on consumer return policies and supply chain coordination. Omega **45**, 57–70 (2014)
7. Kim, S., Baek, T.H.: Examining the antecedents and consequences of mobile app engagement. Telemat. Inf. **35**, 148–158 (2018)
8. Yin, C., Ding, S., Wang, J.: Mobile marketing recommendation method based on user location feedback. Hum. Centric Comput. Inf. Sci. **91**(9), 1–17 (2019)
9. Gao, H., Kuang, L., Yin, Y., Guo, B., Duo, K.: Mining consuming behaviors with temporal evolution for personalized recommendation in mobile marketing apps. Mob. Networks Appl. **254**(25), 1233–1248 (2020)
10. Amrouche, N., Pei, Z., Yan, R.: Mobile channel and channel coordination under different supply chain contexts. Ind. Mark. Manag. **84**, 165–182 (2020)

11. Dada, M., Srikanth, K.N.: Pricing policies for quantity discounts. Manage. Sci. **33**, 1247–1252 (1987). https://doi.org/10.1287/mnsc33101247
12. Winter, R.A.: Vertical control and price versus nonprice competition. Q J Econ **108**, 61–76 (1993)
13. Iyer, G.: Coordinating channels under price and nonprice competition. Mark. Sci. **17**, 338–355 (1998). https://doi.org/10.1287/mksc174338
14. Cachon, G.P.: Supply chain coordination with contracts. Handbooks Oper. Res. Manag. Sci. **11**, 227–339 (2003)
15. Yao, D.Q., Yue, X., Wang, X., Liu, J.J.: The impact of information sharing on a returns policy with the addition of a direct channel. Int. J. Prod. Econ. **97**, 196–209 (2005)
16. Kurata, H., Yao, D.Q., Liu, J.J.: Pricing policies under direct vs. indirect channel competition and national vs. store brand competition. Eur. J. Oper. Res. **180**, 262–281 (2007)
17. Huang, W., Swaminathan, J.M.: Introduction of a second channel: implications for pricing and profits. Eur. J. Oper. Res. **194**, 258–279 (2009)
18. Chen, J., Liang, L., Yao, D.Q., Sun, S.: Price and quality decisions in dual-channel supply chains. Eur. J. Oper. Res. **259**, 935–948 (2017)
19. Boyaci, T., Ray, S.: Product differentiation and capacity cost interaction in time and price sensitive markets. Manuf. Serv. Oper. Manage. **5**, 18–36 (2003). https://doi.org/10.1287/msom511812757
20. Haucap, J., Heimeshoff, U.: Consumer behavior towards on-net/off-net price differentiation. Telecomm. Policy **35**, 325–332 (2011)
21. Herbon, A.: Optimal two-level piecewise-constant price discrimination for a storable perishable product. Int. J. Product. Res. **56**, 1738–1756 (2015). https://doi.org/10.1080/0020754320151018451
22. Danzon, P.M.: Differential pricing of pharmaceuticals: theory, evidence and emerging issues. Pharmacoeconomics **36**, 1395–1405 (2018)
23. Raza, S.A., Govindaluri, S.M.: Greening and price differentiation coordination in a supply chain with partial demand information and cannibalization. J. Clean. Prod. **229**, 706–726 (2019)
24. Hess, J.D., Chu, W., Gerstner, E.: Controlling product returns in direct marketing. Mark. Lett. **74**(7), 307–317 (1996)
25. Chu, W., Gerstner, E., Hess, J.D.: Managing dissatisfaction: how to decrease customer opportunism by partial refunds. Manage. Dissatisf. **1**, 140–155 (2016). https://doi.org/10.1177/109467059800100204

Author Index

Printed in the United States
by Baker & Taylor Publisher Services